1176 *Spiritual gifts bestowed*   1 CORINTHIANS, 12

25 After the same manner also he
took the cup, when he had supped,
saying, This cup is the new testa-
ment in my blood: this do ye, as
oft as ye drink *it*, in remembrance
of me.

26 For as often as ye eat this
bread, and drink this cup, [2] ye do
shew the Lord's death till he come.

27 *f* Wherefore whosoever shall eat
this bread, and drink *this* cup of the
Lord, unworthily, shall be guilty of
the body and blood of the Lord.

28 But *g* let a man examine himself, and so let him eat of *that* bread,
and drink of *that* cup.

29 For he that eateth and drinketh unworthily, eateth and drinketh
[3] damnation to himself, not discern-
ing the Lord's body.

30 For this cause many *are* weak
and sickly among you, and many
sleep.

31 For *h* if we would judge ourselves, we should not be judged.

32 But when we are judged we
are chastened of the Lord, that ye
should not be condemned with the
world.

The

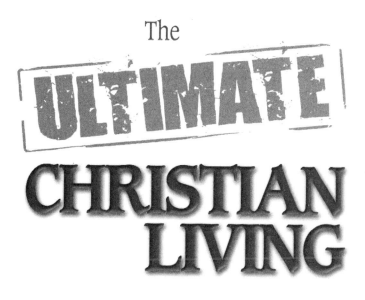

ULTIMATE
CHRISTIAN
LIVING

Faith and Fellowship
Celebrated Through
Stories and Photos

Todd Outcalt
Pastor, Calvary United Methodist Church

Health Communications, Inc.
HCI Books, the Life Issues Publisher
Deerfield Beach, Florida

www.hcibooks.com
www.ultimatehcibooks.com

We would like to acknowledge the writers and photographers who granted us permission to use their material. Copyright credits for interior photographs appear on each photograph and credits for literary work are listed alphabetically by authors' last names. Contact information as supplied by the photographers and writers can be found in the back matter of this book.

Scripture quotations appearing in this book are from the New International Version and the King James versions of the Bible.

Library of Congress Cataloging-in-Publication Data
is available through the Library of Congress.

©2010 Health Communications, Inc.
ISBN-13: 978-0-7573-1453-7
ISBN-10: 0-7573-1453-8

Publisher: Health Communications, Inc.
        3201 S.W. 15th Street
        Deerfield Beach, FL 33442-8190

Cover Design: Justin Rothkowitz
Interior design and formatting: Dawn Von Strolley Grove

To Teri Peluso
Who made all things possible for this book.

To the writers and congregations
we worked with on this book project:

You are gifted people, all.

Is something "Ultimately" important to you?
Then we want to know about it. . . .

We hope you enjoyed *The Ultimate Christian Living*. We are planning many more books in the Ultimate series, each filled with entertaining stories, must-know facts, and captivating photos. We're always looking for talented writers to share slice-of-life true stories, creative photographers to capture images that a story can't tell, as well as top experts to offer their unique insights on a given topic.

For more information on submission guidelines, or to suggest a topic for an upcoming book, please visit the Ultimate website at **www.ultimatehcibooks.com,** or write to: Submission Guidelines, Ultimate Series, HCI Books, 3201 SW 15th St., Deerfield Beach, FL 33442.

For more information about other books by Health Communications, Inc., please visit **www.hcibooks.com.**

Contents

Must-Know Info

Introduction

Through the years I've heard many people use expressions like, "He lives a Christian life" or "She was a good Christian woman." But what does it mean to live as a Christian?

This question is really at the heart of what *The Ultimate Christian Living* is about. As I read through the wonderful essays and testimonies in this book, I discovered that the Christian life is far more wonderful, varied, and beautifully articulated than any single person can express. Living for Christ is, indeed, an adventure that takes people to some amazing places and offers immense blessings.

These experiences and lessons lived with Christ, however, are not always easy or immediate. Sometimes these blessings come only through sacrifice, or pain, or hardship.

Being a pastor for the past twenty-five years, I've heard my share of clichés about the Christian life—and there are plenty to go around. But this book has none of the trite formulas or slick platitudes often associated with Christian living. Rather, in these pages you will discover many testimonies that integrate personal faith with daily life experience. Others offer up wonderful, even painfully beautiful, expressions of Christian faith as experienced through difficulty or illness. And, yes, there is enough humor and joy in these pages to communicate God's love with a smile or a chuckle.

In short, this truly is an ultimate glimpse of how God touches and embraces human lives and changes our world with the love of Christ. I know I gained perspective—and certainly grew in my faith—by reading every single one of these personal stories. Written by young and old alike, each one of these stories offered me a glimpse of how another has experienced God's love and grace.

These stories also offer up wisdom from diverse vantage points—be it city or country, large church or small church, tranquility or turmoil—as a testimony to the vastness of God's kingdom and the myriad ways that God works in our own personal circumstances and situations. You will discover new voices and surprising insights about a few of the best-known personalities in the church today, as well as stories about some of the largest churches in America.

But the ultimate blessing of this book is to be found in the witness it provides—a witness to the life-changing grace of God, who makes all things new and heals the broken world. Every page offers encouragement and hope, and anyone who is seeking to live the Christian life will certainly discover a deeper faith through these personal stories.

Reading this book is like listening to a conversation. And from conversation, faith is often discovered.

I know that I have grown in faith in this way.

Years ago, as a young seminary student preparing for pastoral ministry, I was blessed to have an older pastor in my life who served as a mentor and friend. His name was Jeff Davis, and Jeff deeply influenced my faith through his kind words, his wisdom, and his insights. Sometimes, when I was engaged in a lively conversation with Jeff, it was like having a discussion with God—and receiving the benefits of Jeff's experience was a double-blessing.

One afternoon while we were riding in the car after a hospital visitation, Jeff offered up his personal blend of "expert tips" that, he said, would provide me with the energy and stamina needed to make ministry a lifetime work. "You know," he said, "there's nothing too fancy about living for the Lord when you get right down to it. Don't ever get too high on yourself—you have to remember that God makes all things possible, not you! And don't ever get too down on yourself either—because God is your strength and hope and salvation. There's nothing too difficult for God. And finally—get up early, and take an afternoon nap every day to recharge your batteries. See . . . I'm a living testimony!"

Indeed, Jeff had been living for the Lord and taking his naps for nearly fifty years. And he had more energy than I did.

Although Jeff is with the Lord now, I have not forgotten his wisdom (and yes, I do *sometimes* take an afternoon nap). Nor will I soon forget the wisdom I've found in *The Ultimate Christian Living*—insights about prayer, dealing with difficulties, or living the golden rule, in addition to the many expert tips offered up by some of the brightest minds in the church today.

Personally, I'm still trying to figure out what it means to live a Christian life. Some days I think I succeed rather admirably—and at other times, I struggle. I have days when everything falls into place and all is right with the world. And I have other days when it seems the fabric of life is ripping apart. As a pastor, I know this is how every Christian experiences life. Nothing can be taken for granted, and there is enough mystery in our lives to keep us wondering and learning into the twilight of life. We need to listen to each other if we are to grow into the likeness of Jesus—and we often receive His love and grace through the hands, feet, and kind actions of others.

But in the end, I suppose that is why ultimately it is faith that is required to live as a Christian. It is not just our personal experiences that reflect faith in Christ, but also the experiences of others who see God's grace in their achievements and through the struggles they face. And when we learn to listen to each other—and truly hear the faith story that another has to tell—that is when true Christian living spills over into service, generosity, encouragement, and hope.

And I hope you will be blessed by all of the personal stories and the expert tips in *The Ultimate Christian Living*.

Challenges

A Chaplain's Cheer

By Carol McAdoo Rehme

The night receptionist handed me a slip of paper. "The volunteer chaplain would like to meet with you," it read. "This is her extension number."

Her? The hospital chaplain is a woman? I was exhausted after spending a full ten hours supervising my son's third day of intensive therapy at Craig Rehabilitation Hospital. I was not in the mood to explain—for what seemed like the thousandth time—the accident that had brought us here.

"Maybe tomorrow," I muttered, ducking into the crisp night air. Street lamps lit my path across the pedestrian walkway and cast shadows as immense as the worries that weighed heavily on my heart. Overtired, I fumbled with the unfamiliar locks of the guest-apartment door, and tumbled into bed without even washing my face or brushing my teeth.

The next morning a different receptionist handed me another slip of paper. "The hospital chaplain wants to . . . "

"I know," I sighed, "I know. Is she in now?" She opened her mouth to answer but nodded and pointed instead. As I turned my head, I was startled by the middle-aged woman lumbering toward me. Her walk was lopsided, like a gate swinging on one hinge, her eyes were skewed, and even her arms seemed twisted, out of her control. She looked like she could have been one of the patients. Her smile radiated warmth as she greeted me.

"Are you Kyle's mother?"

I nodded, trying to recover from my complete surprise.

"What a wonderful, charming son you have! I could hardly wait to meet the person who brought him into the world." Although her words were slurred, I understood the message, and it melted the icy knot that had been lodged in my stomach for weeks. Here was someone who knew my son only *after* his head injury—and liked what she saw.

"Let's sit," she said, pointing toward two chairs. We sat and talked . . . and talked.

So began my brief relationship with Patty Cooper—lay chaplain, confidante, teacher, and friend. Her regular visits to Kyle cheered him. Her regular visits to me gave me hope—a hope she spread as generously as her encouragement in a facility that treated only the most severe brain and spinal injuries.

As I dealt with my son's infirmities and my own doubts, I came to rely on the unique mixture of relentless optimism and calm acceptance conveyed by Patty and so many others at Craig. I needed both optimism and acceptance as I grieved over the losses and adjusted to the countless changes.

She complimented Kyle's attitude and each small success as he worked hard to rebuild his body and to walk again. She encouraged my involvement and soothed my maternal fears. And she shared her personal story when I asked how she found herself volunteering in a place where heartache reigned supreme.

"I wanted to have a baby," she said simply.

Twenty-five years earlier, during a straightforward exploratory surgery of her fallopian tubes, she was given an overdose of nitrous oxide gas. It initiated an unexpected path in Patty's life. The resulting complications and permanent disabilities read like an index of medical terms: cardiac arrest, anoxia, hypoxic brain surgery, a forty-day coma, paralysis, peripheral blindness, impaired speech, and cognitive lapses.

Patty awoke from the initial surgery months later to discover she was a patient at this very facility. After many long months, she relearned the basics: how to walk and talk, how to feed and dress herself, how to brush her hair and teeth, and how to tend to her most personal needs. In the meantime, Patty's husband chose a different path—with a different woman—for himself.

"You don't seem bitter," I pointed out. "And you ended up here by choice." After a month, I sometimes still struggled with the heart-wrench of each patient's pain and problems that I witnessed on a daily basis. I wondered, *How could she do it, night and day, year after year?*

The crooked smile that I had come to love lifted a corner of her mouth and crinkled her tender eyes. "Yes, I want to be here," she responded. And then Patty taught me a powerful lesson about change and acceptance.

"Years ago, I had planned to conceive one perfect child of my own to love, but God showed me that love doesn't seek perfection." She paused to brush away a single, crystalline tear and nodded toward the row of wheelchairs, walkers, and weights that lined the corridor.

"And now . . . now I voluntarily walk through these doors each day for a more important reason: to share my love with all of His children."

Less Is Best!

By Linda E. Allen

"There but for the grace of God go I" is a phrase that inspires gratitude in many of us when we see someone less fortunate. I've often thought that in my work with the Aymara Indians of Bolivia. I'm a Spanish interpreter for Volunteers in Mission (VIM) medical and construction teams. Bolivia is the poorest country in South America—by economic standards, that is. But I've learned that in spite of their material poverty, they are rich in what really matters: family, friends, and the simple things in life.

My discovery of their wealth began when my minister invited me to travel with the VIM team from our church. The team travels annually to Bolivia. He promised adventures like crossing a river on a raft, sleeping on straw mats, outside latrines (if we were lucky), and working with people in extreme poverty—all in the beautiful Andes mountains. I decided to take the challenge, though I have to admit my reason for going was more selfish than spiritual. I wanted to escape a dream job that had turned into a nightmare. I was determined to use this two-week "getaway" to evaluate the situation from a distance and to decide whether to stay or leave the job.

The trip was everything my minister had promised and more. We crossed that river on a raft and as extra excitement, pulled the bus out of the mud using a human chain when the bus didn't quite make it off the raft. We ate simple basic food, slept on straw mats on the floor, went to bed when the sun set and got up when it rose the next morning. It was a mind-refreshing, soul-cleansing, and life-changing retreat. I loved it! We worked in poverty I could not have imagined without seeing and experiencing it.

To my surprise, the people were happy—even joyful—in spite of their lack of life's basic necessities that we take for granted. They were grateful for our gifts of small toys and trinkets for their children, baseball caps, T-shirts, and the time we spent with them. Inner peace, serenity, and faith showed deep in their eyes and in their daily activities. I wanted what they had. With all my material stuff, I was miserable. It wasn't a pretty picture when I faced myself in the mirror and asked, *What's wrong with you, girl?* The answer? My priorities were upside down. I was more spoiled and more selfish than I wanted to admit. The challenge: to put my priorities in the proper order. For this to happen, my thoughts and value system had to change.

I returned home and left my job—now an easy decision to make because I knew what I wanted. A fancy job with all the perks and accompanying stress no longer fit my needs and dreams. Giving up a regular salary with benefits for financial insecurity and no definite job made my family and friends question my sanity and career move, which appeared to them a downward move. Today, I'm happily self-employed. I have less materially and financially, but I have more spiritually. I'm happy and thankful for all

I have—especially family and friends. And, because I'm happier, everyone around me is also. After all, it's more fun to share happiness than self-induced misery.

By the grace of God, I have been blessed and taught by the poor. I had to travel to Bolivia to recognize how blessed I am. Through that experience I recognized the abundance that surrounds me. I return every year for a review lesson on what is really important in life. The bigger reason I return, though, is that I get to work with and serve people I have come to love, my second family. Within the word "blessing" is the small word "less." In a far-off, unfamiliar land high in the Andes, away from our consumer-driven culture, I learned that I can live abundantly—with less.

Prison Break

By Lynne Gentry

After a long and unproductive church staff meeting, I trudged to my desk. I'd been unable to make any progress on the pile of work already cluttering my desk, and now more had just been added to my very full plate. Mounting ministry obligations surrounded me like iron bars.

The secretary buzzed me on the intercom. With an exhausted sigh, I dumped the list of this week's countless details on my desk. Sunday would be here before I knew it, and I would not be ready.

I punched the blinking button. "What do you need, Barbara?"

"Can you come to the lobby?" The receptionist's voice sounded urgent. "We have a . . . situation."

Situation is church code for *someone no one wants to deal with.* Situations always meant more work for those on the lower end of the church-hierarchy scale. Situations meant more work for me.

I stomped to the lobby, fully intending to duck anyone's attempt to add another commitment or obligation to my weary shoulders. I rounded the corner, and seated in front of the receptionist's desk was a young woman, paper-thin with stringy, over-processed hair. I stopped abruptly. I knew panhandler trouble when I saw it. This girl was as skittish as a cornered animal and had the look of someone with a blazing past and a bleak future. I'd spent eight years living in a parsonage situated on Hobo Highway so I knew the signs. Vagrants and homeless people traveled that coastal road, migrating south in the winter, heading north in the summer. They'd stop at the church looking for money, food, or any handout they could get. If they couldn't rouse someone at the building, they'd hightail it across the church parking lot and pound on our parsonage door.

After countless payouts, the only tangible reward I had to show for my benevolent efforts was a wary distrust of mankind. No doubt this girl, with the tattoo on her neck, wanted something for nothing, and I was in no mood to be taken again.

I stepped into the room determined to keep this short and sweet. "Hi. I'm the preacher's wife. Can I help you?"

"My probation officer said I need to find a church home." She pulled a battered paper Bible out of her purse. "A lady gave me this in prison and when I read it, I found the Lord. But I've got a lot of questions. I'd sure appreciate it if someone could help me study on it some more. Could you help me?"

Something about the way she held on to that dog-eared Bible—desperate, as if it were some sort of lifeline—dissolved the dismissive words that had been waiting on the tip of my tongue. "Me?"

"Only if you have time." She tugged the hem of a skimpy shirt that failed to cover her bare midriff. "I'm a three-time felon, a drug addict, and I'm having trouble with relapsing. You might not want to waste your time on me."

None too kindly, I spat out, "What's your name?"

"Stella. Stella the Felon."

"Well, Stella the Felon, be here next Wednesday." What was I thinking? I didn't have time for this. Why had these words popped out of my mouth? "Four o'clock. And don't be late or stand me up."

"Oh, I won't. I'll be here."

I spun and returned to me office, my mind replaying what I'd just said and the uncannily honest conversation I felt I'd just had with an ex-con. She'd not tried to hide the truth nor had she asked for a dime. And for some unexplainable reason, I believed the smile lighting a face that was probably very pretty under that makeup. This woman would do what she said she'd do. I pulled my Bible out from under the rubble on my desk and dusted it off, ashamed at how long had it been since I'd actually had my head in the Word.

As the week progressed, I wondered if getting material together for Stella was another waste of my time. I could have been wrong about her. She might not even show up. But come Wednesday afternoon, Stella appeared at my office door. She had the same grubby Bible in hand and an expectant grin on her face.

I gathered up the study aids I had prepared and ushered her into the nearest conference room. I sat across the table from her. She was jumpy and struggled to remain focused. "You lie to me about anything, especially about whether or not you're using again, and we're through. Understand, Stella?"

She nodded and we set to work. Within seconds, I realized she already had a keen understanding of Jesus. That she'd been saved by His power bubbled from her pores. "So what do you want from me, Stella?"

She pointed to her Bible. "Tell me the whole story." Then she flipped to Genesis. "Like what about this guy in the boat?"

"Noah? You want to know about Noah?" I couldn't believe it. She wanted me to explain basic Sunday school stories. This would take years. "Stella, I don't have time . . . " I stopped. I couldn't remember the last time I'd seen such hunger to know God in someone's eyes.

With a smothered sigh, I put away my planned study curriculum and opened my Bible to Genesis. Chapter by chapter, Stella and I began to tackle the ancient stories of faith, investigating the victories and failings of one biblical hero after another. Cautiously, Stella began to discuss her mistakes. She devoured any hope of a better and forgiven life that the Word had to offer. Like water transforms a germinating seed, the power of God's love slowly transformed Stella. She blossomed before my eyes. She could sit still for longer and longer periods of time. Her eyes sparkled and the luster had returned to her hair. Her zeal was contagious, infecting me with the same optimism.

In the months that followed, Stella and I logged many hours together. We went to lunch. We went for coffee. We went clothes shopping. We went to probation. To counseling. To the job corps. We laughed. We cried. We worked through several relapses and a couple of times when she tried to kill herself. We grew closer to the Lord and very close to each other.

One Wednesday, after finishing our study time, Stella looked up from her Bible with tears in her eyes. "Speaking of God, I think you're one of God's little people."

"What do you mean?"

"You know, one of His helpers."

"How so?"

"I thought prison was all I deserved. That no one could love someone like me, nothing could redeem all the bad I've done. But I was wrong. I've been out of prison for nearly a year, but you've helped me see Christ. You've set me free."

I glanced at the small untouched stack of work on my desk. Somehow in the midst of all the time I'd given to Stella, the Lord had given me the ability to get twice the work done in half the time. Investing in someone else had blessed me. My passion and energy had been restored and more important, God had reminded me of why I'd chosen to follow Him in the first place. His work was not the ball and chain I had made it, but rather a wonderful way of life, one that could and would bless others. Who would have thought that the biggest blessing of living in Christ would be the change in my life?

Over the lump in my throat, I said, "No, Stella. God used you to set me free."

A year later, Stella and I are still studying together. We consider ourselves works in progress. We are confident that He who began this good work in us will carry it out to completion in His time.

Preparation

By Jerry Hendrick

During her sophomore year in high school, my daughter Ashley was given an assignment to write a fictional short story. Ashley chose to write her story about a female teenage tennis player who "got" cancer, and she titled her story "The Last Match." In the story the girl's cancer was terminal, and as her health got worse, she became too sick to continue playing the game she loved. As the girl's health deteriorated, she prayed to God that she would become strong enough to play just one more tennis match before she died. In Ashley's story, the girl achieved her dream to play one final match, and shortly thereafter the cancer took her life.

What is especially amazing about this story is that Ashley wrote it almost one full year before any evidence of her own cancer was discovered. She had no earthly way of knowing when she chose her topic and wrote her story that cancer would very soon become much more than just a high school writing assignment. Ashley was diagnosed with osteosarcoma (bone cancer) ten months after she wrote her story, and as a result of this diagnosis; our family went through the most difficult but amazing year of our collective lives.

Prior to the onset of cancer, Ashley had been a promising high school tennis player, hopeful of earning a college scholarship and continuing her career at the next level. In an effort to save her life though, she chose to have her leg amputated, thereby giving up that dream. There were many other challenges Ashley and our family faced during the period we spent "living" at the hospital. There were times of despair where sickness and pain were all we knew, and times of hope, where we could tell that God was with us and that He had a wonderful plan for her life. Overall, it was an incredible chapter of our lives we never would have chosen, which ultimately caused us to be changed for the better.

Over time, my wife, Beth, and I have come to believe that Ashley's story about the tennis player with cancer provides an example of God preparing her for what she would later have to face in her own life. With the writing of the story, it seems that Ashley was led to consider in a very personal way something that most kids her age would have a difficult time imagining. She thought about a young female athlete's mortality and how a life can be changed in an instant by cancer. She also thought about the importance of family and friends, and the beautiful role that God's people through church can play in helping a person make it through something that would be so much harder to handle alone. Even though it was almost a year after Ashley wrote her story before her own cancer was discovered, it seems that God was already preparing her emotionally for her own difficult journey. He was laying the spiritual groundwork.

One of the lessons we can take from our family's experience is that we must always trust that God will give us the strength we need to stand up to all of the challenges we will face in life. We must also have faith to know that whenever those challenges do come our way, He will always be with us. I thank God for His preparations and His presence in Ashley's life. We would never have made it to where we are today without Him.

A Mountain of Fear

By Kristen Feola

There we were, hanging on the side of a mountain, suspended from a single piece of climbing gear. We were more than 500 feet off the ground, climbing our first multi-pitch route, and we were in trouble.

My husband, Justin, and I had been rock climbing for about two years, and our trip to Yosemite was the fulfillment of a dream for both of us. The guidebook said "The Nutcracker" would take two to three hours to climb. We had already been on the route for about four to five hours, with the most difficult part of the climb still to come. On a multi-pitch route, you have to stop occasionally to establish what is known as a belay station, where you break down your equipment, set up your gear, and start the climbing process all over again. Given our inexperience with multi-pitch climbing, we neglected to factor in the extra time it would take us at each belay station. Then, to make matters worse, halfway through the climb the wind began blowing so hard that it was difficult to hear each other. This forced us to slow down to avoid making a fatal mistake.

After hours of climbing in the heat of summer, we were hot,

tired, frustrated, hungry, and dehydrated. I felt waves of panic sweep over me, realizing that with one wrong move, we would plummet to the ground. My mind kept imagining what would happen if the single cam that was holding us broke loose. Thoughts of death flooded my mind. When my husband, who is usually very laid-back and calm, was obviously worried, I knew the situation was serious. At one point, I honestly didn't think we were going to make it. I began to pray. *God, help us! I'm so scared. I don't want to die like this. Please do something. We need You.*

I heard them before I could see their faces. Their voices were barely audible over the roar of the wind, but the people climbing above us were asking Justin if we needed help. I remember thinking about Hebrews 13:2 and was convinced that our rescuers were angels in disguise. I breathed a huge sigh of relief. We were going to be okay. *Thank you, God,* I prayed.

Once we reached the summit, I sat in a daze for several minutes, just happy to be on solid ground. I didn't even want to move. My whole body was still a little shaky from the whole ordeal. It was the closest to death that I'd ever been. But, death was not God's plan for us that day. He sent those two climbers to help us—I have no doubt about that.

He also taught me that when consumed with fear, I always have two choices. One, I can allow my mind to torture me by replaying the fear over and over again until I'm paralyzed by it. Or two, I can throw myself at the Lord's feet, confess my fear, and trust Him to give me victory.

After our near-death experience, we didn't have any desire to climb. We loved the challenge and adventure of rock climbing.

However, we'd encountered a little more adventure than we'd planned on. Personally, I was more than ready to give up climbing for good. That's when God spoke directly to my fear. He reminded me that as His child, I am destined to enjoy His perfect peace. He assured me that He could help me conquer any fear in my life by trusting completely in Him.

The rock that sits on my computer desk today was taken from a multi-pitch climb we did only two days later. We knew that if we didn't get back out there soon, we might never climb again. After what we had endured, the idea of being hundreds of feet off the ground did not appeal to me at all. But, I didn't want fear to take control of this area of my life. So, despite our hesitation, we forced ourselves to climb. We made it to the top without any problems, and the view was absolutely breathtaking! While walking down the mountain after the climb, I picked up the rock as a visual reminder of the powerful lesson God taught me on that trip. He showed me that in order to experience freedom from anxiety, I must surrender the fear to Him and believe He will deliver me.

When anxious thoughts invade your mind, you, too, have a choice. You can dwell on the fearful thoughts and make yourself a nervous wreck. Or, you can choose to pray and ask the Lord for strength. Now, since every good life lesson encourages you to take immediate action, here is an opportunity to take your first step. Ask Him to show you any areas of fear in your life. Tell Him that you will trust in Him and Him alone to give you victory. Then, sit back—and watch Him move your mountain of fear.

The Journey

By Sara Joy Baker

My husband, Bill, is a pastor, and he and I grew up in a time when homosexuality was seldom mentioned—and then only in hushed and darkened tones. In our ministry, we followed the general consensus of Christendom that it was a heinous sin and certainly unnatural in God's order of things. There was no need for study or discussion on the subject, only reminders from time to time that the Bible condemned such acts as demonstrated in the story of Sodom and Gomorrah. I had never known a homosexual and did not anticipate any direct contact with one.

When our seventeen-year-old son, Matthew, "came out" to us a few days prior to his high school graduation, our immediate reaction to his announcement was shock, followed by denial. "You're not a homosexual, you can't be! You've just gotten in with the wrong crowd, and they've convinced you that you're gay," we argued.

He insisted no one "convinced" him he was gay, that his friends had helped him understand who he really was, and that he had always been different from other guys. Many hours passed as we listened to his pain—the rejection, confusion, and hopelessness he had experienced over the years.

We wanted desperately to do something to turn this tide of unthinkable misery pressing upon our hearts. We grasped at straws. Surely a wise counselor could help Matthew see how he needed to seek help and direction. Matthew revealed that he had already talked with several counselors and was convinced it would make no difference. To please us he agreed to try once more, but that, too, proved to be a dead end.

It never entered our minds to disown or alienate him, as we learned many parents feel compelled to do. He had been entrusted to us by a loving God. He would always be part of us and our son. With heavy hearts, we began the journey with him, all the while seeking answers, engaging with him in deep discussion, and praying—always praying. We tearfully pleaded with God to intervene and to change our son. As we continued to seek answers, troubling questions arose in our minds. Did we somehow fail our son? I read books on the subject written in the forties and fifties, and the conclusions only added to my distress. The consensus of opinion of many psychologists at that time pointed to us: overprotective or over-dominant mothers, and absent or weak-willed fathers were the main cause for homosexual sons. For awhile, both Bill and I succumbed to the "blame game," but we soon realized such futile thinking would produce nothing but added torment.

Our greatest fear from the onset of this journey was that Matthew was not really "saved," despite having been raised going to church, summer camps, and other youth meetings. As a young child he accepted Christ as his Savior and was baptized. Later in his teen years he made a recommitment to the Savior. If he truly loved Christ and belonged to Him, how could Matthew live as a homosexual? I sorely needed answers, and day after day I would pray for my son, for myself and my husband, and for peace of mind. God was listening, and after a time gave me assurance that Matthew was forever His child. That was probably the place in our journey where Bill and I began to rethink the traditional viewpoints of the Christian community toward homosexuality.

Many years later, Bill and I were called to minister where gays and lesbians were an integral part of the membership. Many of them had previously held leadership positions in various churches but had been expelled when their homosexuality became known. For some, those experiences were so painful that they had succumbed to alcoholism and drugs. They felt lost and forsaken by the God they had loved and served. At the beginning we had our own prejudices and misconceptions to overcome, but it was not long before we ceased thinking of these members as "different." Instead, we saw them as people who loved God and desired to know Him better. Our purpose as God's messengers was to love them and lead them to Christ. We accepted everyone as He accepted them and us through faith and His grace. We found them hungry for "the Word" and eager to carry the message of Christ's love and forgiveness to others like them.

Bill preached the same lessons to them as he had delivered to other congregations over the previous forty-five years; mainly, that we are all sinners in need of God's forgiveness, and when we accept Jesus' sacrificial death as our only hope, He saves us and empowers us to walk in the light of His word as we go through this life. I recall one evening following Bible study in our home when one of the ladies hugged us and said, "I've prayed so long for someone like you to come along and show us that God really cares. Thank you."

As our ministry with them came to a close, one truth became painfully clear. There is a price to pay when one attempts to love as Jesus loved. He was criticized and maligned for touching the untouchables, eating and drinking with sinners, and extending forgiveness and mercy to prostitutes. How can we expect any less when we show Christian love to the outcasts of our time? Many of our former minister friends and co-workers could not accept our work and outlook as being from God. We became "unclean" to them because we dared to "touch" those they considered unclean before God.

We are now retired, and we look back on our spiritual journey and marvel at what God did in revealing His will to us. We certainly do not claim to have absolute answers in the matter of homosexuality. Yet, as we look back on the gift of our son, we do understand the "why" a little better. Through the Holy Spirit, the "what" of the Gospel message was made clearer, and finally, the "when" reminds us our journey is ongoing.

Eat This Bread

By Lisa Finch

The moment I stepped into his classroom in the parochial school, my son Matthew, who had autism, made a beeline for me. He was clearly distressed. Matthew's autism had severely stunted his ability to use expressive language, but he made his wishes clear that day. "Go home!" he insisted as he pulled me toward the door.

But we couldn't leave. His second grade teacher needed to speak with me. "I was wondering if you wanted Matthew to make his First Holy Communion," she said.

Yes. No. Maybe. I didn't know.

Our family was unable to attend church together because of Matthew's inability to sit through Mass. When his teacher asked me this question, many more questions crashed in on me, and as Matthew tugged on my hand, I tried to sort through them. How much would Matthew get from this? How much would he understand? How would we get him to participate?

"Go home!" he said again.

"We could try," suggested his teacher, who was good at ignoring his verbal outbursts.

"Okay, let's do it," I told her as Matthew led me out of the classroom.

Getting Matthew to his First Communion would take a lot of work and dedication from everyone involved, but one of the things I hoped to gain from this experience was that we, as a family, might actually go to church together.

There was no time to lose as we began our preparations for the big day. We were blessed with a supportive school, including the teacher, educational assistants, principal, and Matthew's classmates. Our parish priest, Father David, was an added blessing. He encouraged the process and understood that it might take a lot of practice and a long time before, or even if, Matthew would receive the Eucharistic bread in his hands, and then in his mouth.

Eat this bread. I could hear the words, and I so hoped that one day Matthew would share, too.

Matthew used expressive language at the level of a three-year-old, so he couldn't tell me what he thought about many things. Perhaps that was the greatest burden of all. I had to accept that perhaps he wouldn't understand the sacrament at all. On the other hand, maybe he would, but he could not tell us.

"I'm not sure how much Matthew will understand," I said to Father David.

"How much does any seven-year-old really understand about this? It takes time," he told me gently.

With everyone's blessing, we began on our journey. We'd already embarked on a journey of sorts, the journey of acceptance and love of our child with the challenges he faced through autism.

But this would involve an entire parish. How would they react?

How should we proceed?

We took a lot of pictures. Pictures of the church, of Father David, of people lining up for communion. I made a social story—a book with lots of pictures, written in easily understandable language that explained exactly why we went to communion and what it means for us. I also explained the correct behavior in a place of worship.

I often joined the class on the days they walked to church to practice for their big day. I watched as the teacher and the students welcomed Matthew to stand beside them while Father David showed them the chalice that would hold the wine and the paten that would hold the bread at the altar. It always amazed me how mindful they were of Matthew's ability to see what was happening.

"See what Father has in his hands, Matthew?" one of his classmates asked.

We practiced. A lot. At home. At church. We started attending church as a family. We made picture strips that showed Matthew what to expect. One picture strip showed "First church, then treat." He loved going to the store after Mass and picking out a candy bar or ice cream. The other picture strip had the words "quiet" at the far left, "talking voice" in the middle, and "loud" at the end. We had a little yellow dot under "quiet," to show Matthew how he should be in church.

Sometimes when I showed him the strip he yelled "quiet" at the top of his lungs. It made me cringe at first. He was loud, and we felt like all eyes were on us sometimes. This was an adjustment for everyone, both in our family and in our church.

When people saw me in town, several surprised me by telling me what a great job we were doing with Matthew. It brought tears to my eyes.

"He's not too disruptive?" I'd ask. I always worried that he was.

"No, not at all. Besides, how will he ever get used to going if you don't take him? You're doing great. Keep it up." These and similar words of encouragement made me realize how truly blessed my family was. Soon, people greeted Matthew in church with a "high-five"—his favorite greeting—and said hello to him. He often ignored them unless prompted to say hello, but they continued to greet him anyway.

First Holy Communion took place in two parts: family day and communion for the entire class. Family day was comparatively easy for us. We went to church, although Matthew hated his suit and tie, and squirmed in his seat. After church, we had a luncheon at our house for our family and friends. Matthew immediately changed into more comfortable clothes and joined in the fun. The day was lovely and warm, and Matt and his cousins, his brother, Ben, and sister, Hailey, ran around outside and enjoyed the food and the company.

The class-wide communion day was more stressful. My husband had been called into work, so it was just me and the three kids. Back in his suit and tie, Matthew really kicked up a fuss. He wanted no further part of the fancy attire.

When we arrived at church, I knew Matthew could not join in the group picture. He'd already been complaining to go home. We were all hot in our dress-up clothes and it seemed to take forever for Mass to begin. I wanted to enjoy this event, but Matthew's insistent pulls on my hands wore me down.

I began to wonder why I had done any of this. Was Matthew gaining anything here or was it just for me? Would church ever be anything less than a chore? Maybe we should go back to our splintered schedule going to church in shifts.

We made it through Mass, and Matthew took the bread in his hands but would not eat it. I suspect, in his mind, he had done his part. Before mass ended, Hailey whispered to me "Are we staying for cake and juice afterward?" I looked at Matthew, who was sweating in his little pressed white shirt and tie. He was uncomfortable and itching to leave.

"I don't think so, Honey, I'm sorry." I could see that Hailey was disappointed. But I also knew this was Matthew's day. *If* he made it to the end of Mass (and it seemed like a big *if*) he'd be rewarded by going home and changing into shorts and a T-shirt.

After Mass, the congregation made their way into the hall to celebrate, and we slipped out. Once at home, we all changed into something more comfortable. We'd made it. We hadn't participated as much as the other children and their parents, but we'd done the best we could.

About forty-five minutes later the doorbell rang.

One of Matthew's classmates was at the door. In his little hands, he held a paper plate with a piece of cake from the church reception. "Here," he said. "I thought Matthew might like this."

Matthew had not taken the communion bread, but I knew he was blessed anyway. In so many ways. And so were we.

The Storm Within

By Diana M. Amadeo

It's happening again. All signs indicate an impending cognitive shift. The result of this electrical short circuit in my brain can resemble a profound panic attack or an intense "senior moment." As my neurologically diseased body slows down, my thoughts can accelerate erratically and then abruptly halt. Like electricity through a frayed wire, neurological impulses and perceptions sometimes get through clearly, sometimes jumbled, sometimes in hyperdrive, and often impulses don't get through at all. Normal daily sprinkles of incoming information can be perceived as a torrential downpour of terrifying awareness. Or, I have no recall, no matter how hard I concentrate. Unimportant trivia mixes with items of substance and becomes impossible to differentiate and prioritize. A previous gentle flowing stream of intelligence becomes a dangerous swirling flood of overwhelming data. Without warning, information overload can burst its banks in raging fury. Or frustration from an inability to perform simple mental tasks sets in. Either way, I am swept into a whirlpool of fear and confusion. . . .

Years ago when I worked as a registered nurse, I recognized that cognitive dysfunction can affect a patient's quality of life even more so than the physical symptoms of disease. Neuropsychological assessments have become an essential portion of the overall evaluation of the brain-injured patient. Now, as I live with the results of brain lesions of multiple sclerosis (MS), I find myself looking over those previous words and going, "Huh?" Big words, medical explanations, and complex terminology are of no assistance to those who live with mild cognitive dysfunction. It's not that we are stupid, it's just that occasionally the simplest things can be a bit confusing.

In this fast-paced world, the information faced daily by any given individual can be mind-boggling. Becoming swamped with data can be difficult for the average person; for the person with cognitive dysfunction, it can be absolutely incapacitating. I am only doing about half of what I was doing before the latest exacerbation of my MS. That's a fraction of the level of activity expected for someone my age. Yet, I am overwhelmed. Things that I need to do are jumbled in my head. It's impossible to make any sense of it all, yet everything must get done.

The medical term for any neurological, cognitively impaired incident is "flooding." It is the inability to prioritize and implement a series of simple tasks or thoughts. I am flooding. Worse, I am drowning. I could be a walking medicine cabinet from all the meds that I have been offered to cope with this, and some in fact, help me gain some ground. But what has given me the greatest sense of control is doing all that I can myself, before finally surrendering when I absolutely cannot continue.

So I take deep breaths to calm the panic, try to focus on lists, and invoke God's help. Outwardly, I get very quiet, then I mentally detach and shut down to everything except the task at hand.

My husband sees that I am currently flooding, so he's posting reminders for me all around the house. (Please keep the porch door shut; turn off the oven; don't throw away new ant traps. . . . But so many notes, so many reminders are discouraging. I feel like an idiot. He's only trying to help. I love him and know that he will pick up the pieces of what I can't get done, and in the end, everything will be all right.

But sometimes I forget how to tread water.

When I can no longer strike items from the "to do" list, I quiet myself and close my eyes. In this meditative state, I surrender to a Higher Power. Almost immediately I feel gentle hands settle upon my head. Panic subsides. There is a feeling of absolute trust. All will be well. Soon, I am wrapped in the Spirit's wings. There is calm and peace within.

And I am floating, not drowning, on this sea of confusion.

Santo Domingo Sunrise

By Terri Elders

When I was a Peace Corps volunteer, I was an education promoter with a social service agency in the remote high desert of western Dominican Republic. After a particularly frenzied Friday visiting volunteer-run preschools, I stopped at the post office in San Juan de la Maguana to pick up my mail and paused at a patio café to read it. To celebrate the close of the week I had an icy Presidente (the local beer) and my favorite snack, a basket of fried plantains.

I shuffled through my correspondence and saved the best for last, setting aside a letter postmarked Antigua, Guatemala. I glanced at the newest edition of *Newsweek*, mailed weekly to volunteers the world over. I decided the next time I got to Santo Domingo, I'd take it to the Epiphany Church for Father Luis. Next, I read a note from a hometown friend in California. She wrote how much she envied me every time she saw Club Med ads on television. I must be having a marvelous time in the D.R., a true island paradise. I smiled. I worked with women who lived in mud huts, and carried water from the river. They cooked vats of beans and rice on makeshift stoves made of rocks in their yards.

I was hours away from the nearest beach by "chicken bus." I might be on an island, but I was far from paradise!

Finally I opened the gauzy blue international airmail envelope, and read that my boyfriend of a decade had met someone else. They would marry in May. I sat stunned, tears trickling down my cheeks. Instead of the usual *salsa* or *meringue*, the café that afternoon was playing an Air Supply tape. So as I read my *Dear Jane* letter, I soaked in the haunting chorus of "All Out of Love." All out of love! I guessed I was . . . and all out of faith. My dreams for the future had just dissolved in the wilting heat of the Dominican afternoon. For so long I'd prayed for a happy ending to this relationship. How could God let me down? I felt as if the sun had set on my world forever.

I finally gathered up my mail, stuffed it in my tote bag, and stumbled toward the house to the room I rented from a Dominican family. I threw some clothes into my duffle bag, scribbled a note for my landlady, and galloped to the bus depot to catch the last evening *guagua* for Santo Domingo. I had to see Reverend Luis. I needed to ask him how to prevent bitterness from finding a permanent home in my heart.

Though I'd not been a regular churchgoer since childhood, I always attended the 9:00 AM English service on Sundays. Reverend Luis, the interim pastor, a priest from Puerto Rico, possessed a keen wit, a sparkling smile, and an abiding penchant for peace. We'd met on one of my library forays, when I saw him eyeing my tote bag with a recent copy of *Newsweek* sticking out the top. I knew that English language magazines sold out quickly in the few stores that carried them. I promised to save my copies for him and deliver them when I came to town.

As soon as the bus stopped near Peace Corps Headquarters on Avenida Bolivar, I dumped off my duffle bag in the volunteers' lounge and headed for the church. Perhaps Father Luis would still be in his rectory. I had my *Newsweek* in hand.

Praise the Lord, I murmured to myself, as I caught him just as he prepared to lock the doors of the parish hall for the evening.

"Could I have a minute?"

"Child, you look as if you've lost your best friend. Come on inside."

He listened patiently as I spilled the story of how I had loved this man in Guatemala for nearly a decade, through our early days together in California, through another Peace Corps stint in another Caribbean country, and how I'd planned to join him in a few months when I'd concluded my service in the D.R.

"I thought he loved me, too," I concluded, fishing yet another tissue from my tote. I felt a bit foolish, almost as if I were asking the priest to explain why bad things happen to good people. I thought of myself as good . . . at least I was doing good deeds.

"Dear, he may love you, but may need this other woman now. She's there, and you're here," Father Luis finally said. "Romantic love ebbs and flows. But maybe God has another plan for you, and you can count on His love forever."

"Another plan? What could it be?"

"It will unfold," Father Luis said. "Just open your mind and heart and wait. Direction will come."

I thanked the priest and handed him my crumpled *Newsweek*. "Please excuse the wrinkles. It got a little squeezed between two gamecocks on the ride in."

"Sometimes it feels like life is like that," he said. "Sometimes we can get squeezed, too, but God has a way of smoothing things out for us."

The next morning as I strode along El Malecón, I noticed a squadron of husky Dominicans jogging towards me, surrounding a small gray-haired man in blue sweats. As they neared, the man glanced my way and lifted a hand in greeting. I waved back, trying to place his face. He looked so familiar. About a hundred yards later I realized it was former President Jimmy Carter. I'd heard that between his visits to Haiti he'd stayed at the American embassy in Santo Domingo.

I figured it was a sign. If Carter, then seventy, could continue to serve his country, so could I. When I returned to the Peace Corps office I asked the director if he could send a fax to headquarters offering my services to yet another part of the world when my time in the Dominican Republic was finished.

It took God a while to smooth out my life, but He did. I got a chance to serve in the Peace Corps again. And this time it really was in paradise: the Republic of Seychelles in the Indian Ocean. Moreover, after my former boyfriend's new marriage failed, we rekindled a friendship that lasted until the day he died.

My life unfolded in a way I'd never anticipated, just as Father Luis predicted. I eventually married somebody new, somebody who just happened to need me. I probably never would have met him had it not been for the priest's encouragement, and that morning in the Santo Domingo sunrise when I passed Jimmy Carter on the Caribbean shore . . . and regained my faith.

Sustaining Faith

By Linda Mehus-Barber

I t seemed that everyone around me was getting pregnant. But month after month, my mood would plummet as I grabbed a hot-water bottle for the inevitable cramps. There wasn't anything I wanted more in the world than to have a baby. When I hit my thirties, my biological clock began ticking a little more desperately. Oh well, at least I have a loving husband, I would think to myself. I was resigned to life without children, and nothing could rock the life I had created—or so I thought.

Then came an incident that foreshadowed the shattering of the world I knew. I volunteered at the Devonian Gardens, making soap to sell in the gift shop. The humidity was suffocating, and as I measured lye into bags, the dust began to react with the beads of perspiration on my arms. I threw down my scoop, ripped off the rubber gloves, and rushed to the sink to run cold water over my burning arms. Suddenly, the garden shed shook as lightning and thunder ushered in a vicious hailstorm.

"I've got to get home," I gasped. "My husband will kill me if the car gets dented."

I grabbed my backpack, and pulling up the hood of my jacket,

ran to the parking lot, dodging pelting hailstones as I swung open
the door and slipped behind the wheel. I hated driving this fancy
sports car and wished for my old Toyota. With the windshield
wipers unable to keep up, the car zoomed along the back roads
towards home. I fumbled with the crackling radio, trying desperately to tune into a news station, and between the static, I managed to catch something about a tornado—a deadly category F4
tornado had touched down with the roar of a freight train.

There is something sobering about being so close to death and
destruction—you take time to reflect on life. After returning
home safely, I renewed my determination to create a perfect
world, while the dark secrets in my husband's heart rose to the
surface. I was surprised at his lack of response to my hug that
night. It was a wall that I couldn't break through. It would be my
last night living in my dream world, and morning would usher in
an abrupt introduction to reality.

The next morning, my husband drove wordlessly to one of our
regular breakfast spots. The silence was deafening, and the sense
of foreboding was every bit as heavy as the clouds of the day
before the storm.

I knew something was wrong—he had been finding excuses
lately to not come home—but I was completely unprepared for
this conversation. The words tumbled from his mouth just as I
lifted my fork with the first bite of a ham and cheese omelet.

"I want a divorce."

I froze before the fork reached my mouth. There we were in
one of Edmonton's finest hotel restaurants, and he was breaking
this news to me there. I felt like everyone was looking at me as the

hot flush rose through to my head. Suddenly a gut-wrenching lump filled the pit of my stomach, and I could no more eat than swim the ocean. The walls closed in and my lungs ached to breathe. As I grasped the meaning of those words, I knew I had to get out of there. My tears flowed in torrents.

With my life in shambles, I tried to make sense of my existence. My mind twisted around ways I might be able to get him back, make him happy. For several months, I clung to the notion that this was just a trial separation, and that he simply had to come to the realization of what he had lost. But it soon became apparent he had found someone else, and the idea of reconciliation evaporated with the spring winds and gurgling snow water. I finally accepted that I had to face life alone.

I sat at my piano, passionately playing Chopin's *Raindrop Prelude* or the second movement of Beethoven's *Pathetique Sonata*—both pieces helped me to release the pain of my broken heart. It was as if my piano cried for me. Tears flowed freely, and the music blurred on the page. Those were lonely nights. The emptiness echoed in my head long after the final notes drifted off into the darkness.

During those times, and as I hiked through the river valley or cuddled up with my dog, I began to listen more intently to the stirring within my spirit. God was clearly directing my steps, and I knew He was walking beside me. I could now see the cracks and fissures that had caused my marriage to crumble. And even more important, I came to understand that neither a husband, nor children, nor financial ease could fill the void in the heart. Idolatry can take many forms, and I began to see the idols I had worshipped in my blindness.

One night as I was reading, my eyes stopped on Isaiah 48:18: "If only you had paid attention to my commands, your peace would have been like a river." With overwhelming sorrow, crushed by guilt and regret, I wept, wondering what might have happened had I placed God above all else.

But we're never to know what might have been, and God wanted more for me. As I gasped for air between sobs, a voice inside my head whispered, "Romans 8:1." Frantically I flipped the pages, wondering what I might find there. "Therefore, there is now no condemnation for those who are in Christ Jesus." As those words entered my heart, a spark ignited the knowledge of what it means to have a personal relationship with the Creator of this universe. Never in my life have I cried as I did at that moment.

God wasn't finished. "Luke 7:13." *What will I find there?* I wondered, and squinting through my tears, I trembled as I turned to the passage. "When the Lord saw her, his heart went out to her and he said, 'Don't cry.'"

Serenity descended upon me, and I basked in the profound-ness of God's unconditional love. The ache of loneliness, the bitterness of divorce, and the shattered dreams of holding my own child were now in God's healing arms. I could move forward with the certainty that He would show me a better way to love.

Over the years, I began to understand that even as I walked this planet alone, I was reaching into the lives of others. In time, the words from Isaiah 54:1 began to describe my life: "'Sing, O barren woman, you who never bore a child; burst into song, shout for joy, you who were never in labour; because more are the children of the desolate woman than of her who has a husband,' says the Lord.''

No longer did I have the hole in my heart from my childlessness and a deserting husband, but I had come to realize just how rich a life I led. God was my focus, and His presence reminded me that whatever did or didn't happen could not cause my joy to be any less. There was a song in my heart, and I was happy with life just as it was.

And then after nearly ten years of travelling alone, God sent Don into my life. I hadn't considered the possibility of falling in love again; I was content in my singlehood. But God hadn't meant for me to be alone, and on a June day under a cloudless blue sky with my apple tree in glorious bloom, I gathered a bouquet of lilacs and walked toward my waiting groom. We've had our bumps and have walked through a wilderness, but we both seek the Lord hungrily, and we both know that only God can satisfy. I'm not living in a dream world this time; I'm living life to its fullest with a faith that sustains.

Decisions, Decisions

By Cheryl Elaine Williams

The sun warmed my neck as I paced along a quiet walkway, clutching a booklet filled with healing scriptures. "Don't worry about anything," I read out loud from the comforting verse in Philippians 4:7. "Instead, pray about everything. Tell God what you need. If you do this, you will experience God's peace." That was exactly what I'd been doing since I was diagnosed with thyroid cancer just before my fifty-seventh birthday.

Oh, how glad I was to be a believing Christian at that awful moment I received such stunning news. If I didn't have the comfort of my faith, I'm sure I would have fallen apart then and there. *Cancer!* The very word made me shiver. When my physician explained that the biopsy done a week before had come back malignant, my body went numb. My focus narrowed to a very strong realization that I was in a fight for my life.

Jesus, I know you're here with me, I remember thinking. The Lord works through his physicians and medical workers to affect cures, I well knew. I had to trust the Lord to do so now. After all, Jesus had guided me to a concerned doctor who had the latest equipment and had caught this problem early. *Thank you, God, for this mercy.* He is good, all the time, in every way and every day of our precious lives. A calmness spread over my spirit just thinking about the Lord's kindness. Names of friends and acquaintances who had walked the path of cancer and beat it filtered through my head. At the same time, my doctor's soothing voice encouraged me. "This is very treatable. I urge you to stay optimistic."

I could do that. My head was spinning with so many thoughts, but I held on tight to hope. One step at a time, I told myself. At that moment, I found I could ask my doctor coherent questions and therefore begin to participate in my own healing.

I had decisions to make. The doctor wanted me to choose a date for surgery. I had to prepare myself mentally to go under the knife to have my cancerous thyroid removed. Nobody welcomes such a scenario. But the bottom line was that I had decided to work with the doctor in this process and to choose life.

Meanwhile, life had to go on. I wrapped a sweater around my shoulders as a kind of security blanket and carried on with my busy day. Bit by bit, I shared the news with family and friends and made the necessary medical appointments. I attended the next meeting of our local cancer support group at my church. I was eager to exchange information and hear how they coped. Everyone's journey with cancer is different, of course, but it helped so much to talk with others about their own experiences.

That meeting was a blessing. The courage of the attendees kept me strong and helped me keep my chin up. *One step forward, ever onward with the Lord's help* became my marching orders. I stayed in the Word, reading the scriptures and listening to Christian radio and music. I didn't become a basket case; I could still enjoy everyday activities like reading a humorous secular book. And by sharing with others, I learned about a number of other people of all age groups who had also undergone successful treatment for thyroid cancer.

"Here's a phone number," church friends would say, putting me in touch with another survivor. "Stay off the Internet sites," one advised me, "you'll only scare yourself silly."

It helped so much to share. People were giving and helpful. Their examples proved to be a true godsend. Just as I was looking at those survivors for inspiration, I understood that people were looking at me, too, to gauge how I was holding up. The experience taught me something very important. We all want to do important things, to set the world on fire, to make a mark on our society. But sometimes the Lord steps in and says, *I have a new mission for you.* At least that is how it felt for me.

I began to feel very strongly that maybe I'm supposed to show other people how to hold up under bad news. Perhaps my existence has come down to this very poignant life lesson.

So feel free to look to me for inspiration, my friends. Look to me and you'll see that I'm scared about being sick. I'm nervous about going under anesthesia. I don't look forward to an overnight stay in the hospital. Chowing down on Jell-O and broth until I heal isn't very appealing, but I'm holding my own. I'm staying in the Word, singing hymns, listening to Christian radio, and attending services. I'm fairly cheerful, all in all. I take my walks and enjoy the sunshine. The world is a place of great beauty with kind people within it.

A Real Man

By Pam Bostwick

*For the Lord seeth not as a man seeth;
for man looketh on the outward appearance,
but the Lord looketh on the heart.*

—SAMUEL, 16:7

I instinctively moved away and tried not to gag as a grungy, unwashed man staggered onto the bus, his stench assaulting my senses. He was filthy from his shoulder-length greasy, graying hair to his grimy toenail that peeked out of dirty leather sandals. He clutched a box of Girl Scout cookies close to his dingy shirt.

A gawky teenager plopped down next to him and blew smoke in the old man's face.

"Watch yourself!" the old man said as he fanned the air.

The boy reluctantly crushed out the cigarette when he saw the bus driver's disapproving look. "It's supposed to be a free country. I'm legal, eighteen today." He lowered his voice. "I've had a joint and a six-pack already."

The man stared at the boy's unfocused eyes with his own sad, hollow ones. "You're not free if your life is ruined."

"My life is my own business." The boy's words slurred. "I'm a man now."

"A real man quits before it's too late and he can't stop. I've had enough of those in thirty years to make me sick, and you will too."

"I can handle myself. Leave me alone."

The old man's shoulders slumped. He paused and looked away. "So long ago I was young like you, thinking I might conquer the world. I knew I had the booze and smoking under control until I couldn't do without it. I learned to despise it." He peered at the young man steadily. "I hated what it did to me when I got mean. My girl was about your age when I lost her and her mother." He gently caressed the cookie box as he would a child. "It ain't worth it."

Then a light lit up his sallow face. "You want a girlfriend, don't ya, and a good job? Don't do what I done. You don't want to be a no-count bum like me who's nothin' and got nothin' to show for it now. Stay off the stuff." He stood up slowly. His thin body seemed stiff with pain as he shuffled off the bus.

"I do have a girlfriend and a good job," the teen muttered to himself while he pulled his pack of cigarettes out of his pocket, took one out and looked at it. Then he put it back in the box.

Because I got off at the next stop, I didn't know if that boy threw those cigarettes in the garbage. I like to think he did.

From the heart of a real man I'd received an understanding about the brokenness caused by addiction. He showed me more truth than a class lecture would have taught me. The greater lesson in humility I gained was to not judge a man by his appearance, only by his soul. That elderly man is a child of God and maybe his whole purpose for being was to help that one young man. What if his words saved that boy? I wish I could have told him his life wasn't in vain.

Living Your Faith

The Better Choice

By Elaine L. Bridge

"To go to church or to *be* the church—Mary made the better choice."

God spoke these words to me as I was rushing home from one church-related function to prepare for yet another one. He was trying to teach me a lesson through the actions of a friend of mine. The name by which I know her is unimportant. God referred to her as "Mary" because she reminds Him of another Mary in the Bible, one who earned her sister's scorn, because she chose to sit at the feet of Jesus rather than help in the kitchen. Yet Jesus said that Mary made the better choice.

My friend had been on my mind a lot of late because I hadn't seen her much in recent weeks. I've wondered why she hasn't been in church as much as usual. She's missed a lot. There have been so many projects that could have used her hands . . . to hand out free hot dogs and soft drinks at an evangelistic outreach . . . to lay on the sick in body or heart in prayer . . . to wave before the Lord in worship as she leads others to do the same. The church needed her hands, but God needed her heart. Mary made the better choice.

It turned out that she'd been busy. Her days had been full of ministry to others—outside the four walls of our church. She'd moved into a new house just when her nearest new neighbor suffered a crisis with a family member who later died. My friend dried her neighbor's tears and found ways to make her neighbor's younger daughter laugh despite the gloom engulfing her household. She made meals and delivered them, held hands that needed her strength, hugged hearts that were breaking. When she wasn't at her neighbor's side, she was sharing in the pride and joy of a friend whose son was graduating from high school—attending the ceremony and helping prepare for the party that followed. She wept with the sad and laughed with the joyful. She wasn't in church, yet she was in the presence of God. Mary made the better choice.

Where *is* God, anyway? Is He to be found inside the walls of a building or does He live instead inside human temples of His Spirit? If God were in my shoes, I wonder which pair He'd choose to wear? The black sandals suitable for a church service, or the Nike tennis shoes for running His errands? I know for a fact that Jesus would wear the pair that took Him to the people who needed His touch. Sometimes that place is in a body of believers, but often a believer's body has to carry God's healing hand to the place it's needed the most . . . even if that means she has to miss a service or two to get it there. Mary made the better choice.

I believe church attendance is important. God says in His Word, "Let us not give up meeting together, as some are in the habit of doing . . . " (Hebrews 10:25). But God wants me to realize that on any given Sunday there might be two types of "church service" that I have to choose between, a choice that has nothing to do with the volume of the worship music or the time of day at which it occurs. One describes a meeting with other believers for the purpose of worshipping God. The other is an act of helpful activity, the rendering of aid to one who needs it, also as a means for worshipping God. In all my church busyness this past week I chose the former. My friend, in her acts of kindness, chose the latter. Mary made the better choice.

The Neighbor I Can't Wait to Hug in Heaven

By Jeanne R. Hill

When Christians get together, they often talk about who they want to see in heaven. Many have a great theologian in mind. Not me. Right after I encounter the Lord and His disciples, there's a neighbor I can't wait to hug in heaven. I was only five years old when I met the tall, slim woman whose copper-colored hair was turning gray. That big smile that wouldn't quit belonged to Minnie Driscoll.

In 1934 we moved into a house across the street from Minnie in Longton, Kansas, and even though she heard my parents cursing each other loudly during the move in, she came right over to meet us. She invited Mama to "come over for coffee when settled," but I knew Mama would never go.

Mama kept to herself. Our whole family did. And no wonder. The neighbors usually shunned us because Mama and Daddy cuss-fought and threw chairs and dishes at each other daily. Often their fights spilled outside. Life for my eight-year-old sister, Jo, and me was a constant uproar with our parents' fights. The arguments were so frightening that once Jo ran into traffic to distract my parents.

Minnie Driscoll ignored all that and treated Mama in a sweet, friendly manner. Mama tried to remain aloof, but Minnie brought over a pitcher of fresh-squeezed lemonade and a plate of oatmeal cookies. She soon had Mama laughing at stories about Minnie's old hound dog. It wasn't long before Jo and I were allowed to go over to Minnie's porch to play with her dog. Then Minnie talked Mama into having our family attend her frequent chili suppers, where laughter filled the neighborhood.

Come Sunday, Minnie donned a navy blue dress with a white lace collar and wore white gloves. Carrying her Bible and purse she called out a friendly, "I wish you'd come to church with me." When Mama shook her head, Minnie smiled big and waved. "Maybe next time," she'd say, walking on down the street.

"Next time" didn't come until Minnie's church held a revival meeting. Minnie came running over the morning after the opening night, her brown eyes sparkling. "What a great group of chamber musicians has come from Cherryvale for the revival! They are just marvelous and they play for a half-hour every night before the service!" Minnie hugged Mama's shoulders. "Marie, didn't you say you and your father loved to go hear chamber music? You must come hear these men!"

"Oh, yes," Mama said. "Why, I've not heard live chamber music for years!" Mama's eyes lit up like Minnie's.

"Then you and the girls come with me tonight. With your husband carpentering in Dearing this week, we'll make a night of it—just us girls." Mama couldn't resist. She dressed Jo and me in our starched best and we walked ahead of Mama and Minnie for ten blocks to the church. That lilac-scented summer evening was one I will never forget.

The church smelled of furniture polish and the fresh-cut red, yellow, and purple roses that filled the room. The musicians sat in front, just below the polished wood pulpit, and they played the sweetest music I'd ever heard. Mama sat enthralled, her eyes closed while they played what Mama called "classical music" until the last two numbers. Just before the sermon started they played a lively "Turkey in the Straw" and finally "The Battle Hymn of the Republic."

As if his words were part of the last hymn, the pastor rose from his chair and started his sermon with "For God so loved the world, that he gave his only begotten Son, that whosoever believeth in Him should not perish, but have everlasting life" (John 3:16). Something happened to Mama during that sermon. I'd never seen her sit so quiet and thoughtful. At the end of the sermon, the pastor invited people to come up front if their lives weren't what they wanted them to be and to confess their sins and accept Christ as their Savior. I didn't understand that last part but I liked the kindly pastor, and I knew Mama wasn't happy with her life.

I was surprised when Mama quietly handed her purse to Jo and went down front. She knelt at the altar and cried like her heart was breaking. It scared me because Mama didn't cry often, but Minnie slipped into the pew beside Jo and me, hugged us, and reassured us that Mama was all right. "Your mama's crying now will bring her happiness later," Minnie said. "You'll see."

Minnie was right. On the way home, I'd never seen Mama so happy. "Girls, our lives are going to change, starting this very night," Mama told Jo and me. "There will be praying instead of cussing from me."

She kept her word. Of course, our home lives didn't go perfectly. Daddy was still a wild card. But that very night Mama and Minnie taught Jo and me a little prayer that we said nightly ever after. We knelt by our beds and prayed, "Now I lay me down to sleep, I pray the Lord my soul to keep. If I should die before I wake, I pray the Lord my soul to take. Amen." How wonderfully reassuring that prayer was to Jo and me.

That night was the beginning of our Christian experience. Both my sister and I mark it as the most important night of our lives. What a tremendous difference that one woman—Minnie Driscoll—made in our three lives! No wonder I can't wait to hug her in heaven.

Church in the Alley

By Mark Sanders

I was burned out, jaded, mired, and tired in my role as a social worker. I'd been listening to and absorbing clients' traumatic experiences for over thirty years. Even new office furniture could not make these negative feelings go away.

A friend invited me to attend the first service of a new church he was pastoring. I dragged myself to the service. There were two-hundred people in attendance and a choir of approximately fifty. The pastor began his sermon by telling the story of a couple who lived in the house next door, whose child had recently died. He pointed out the window and mentioned that the side of their house was across the alley adjacent to the church. The pastor led the entire congregation and the choir into the alley and asked us to sing at the window; perhaps the couple who'd suffered the loss would come to the window and know that there were people who cared.

While we sang the couple came to the window and expressed their appreciation. Others arrived, too. Children joined us in the singing. So did many adults who had not been present at the church service. A group of gang members wandered into the alley, wondering why so many people were there. They joined in the singing as well.

It felt so good to be in that alley. I wondered, *When was the last time I felt this good about giving purely for the sake of giving?* The answer dawned on me: It was when I was twenty-four years old and first became a social worker. In the alley, I recaptured the essence of why I became a social worker in the first place—helping purely for the sake of helping. I renewed my commitment to my profession that day. I vowed that I would take care of myself so that I could continue to enjoy the gift of giving.

The Hand

By Elaine L. Bridge

I've been a "hand" this summer. I know it was my assignment from God. Not to lend a hand, but simply to be one—His—holding tightly to the hand of a woman I hardly knew before the project began. She was a regular at our church's monthly "Soul Food" services; I knew her only by sight when I learned she'd been diagnosed with cervical cancer. From the moment I heard of her illness, I felt as if her problem had become mine and knew we were to walk through the difficulty together, hand in hand. Not physically, necessarily. In fact, I haven't seen her face-to-face since I asked for her name and address several months ago. But I've been holding her hand in the spirit by mail, in cards and letters and stories I've sent to her on a weekly basis as the months have rolled by. She's changed from an acquaintance I knew only by nickname to a friend I know by heart.

I didn't realize all this initially. I just felt it was necessary to send her encouraging news by mail on a weekly basis, never questioning where that prompting came from, as I knew it was God urging me to write. But this morning He gave me the physical illustration to help me better visualize my role in her recovery.

It's helped me understand how we, who are the body of Christ, are to function in facing the tribulations of the world around us. We are Christ's hands and feet—the vessels He uses to minister to others, and I understand more clearly now the importance of what He's asked me to do.

I'm just His hand. Others have been His feet, driving her to doctors' appointments and other places she needed to be. His voice has spoken spiritual health as well as physical healing through men who've taught her the Word of God in Bible studies and who've offered up prayers on her behalf. Friends around her have seen to her physical needs and filled her cupboards with food. The whole body of Christ has ministered to her in one way or another. But I've been privileged to be His hand.

I realize anew the necessity of completing the task faithfully. If I'm to be His hand holding hers throughout the duration of this illness then it's of vital importance that I not quit . . . because *He* would never let go. The outcome of her treatments in no way changes things either. He would keep her hand clasped firmly in His own until she was safely at heaven's gates, if that's where the road she's traveling should take her.

I am thankful that doesn't seem to be the case. Her excellent progress has been cause for great rejoicing. I know that when she's finally declared "cancer free," God will release me to let go of her hands so we both can clap them in joy and then raise them in praise.

A Place for Love

By Valerie J. Frost

The world watched as the space shuttle exploded, shattering the hearts of the families of those on board and sending our nation into a state of shock. At 8:30 AM in San Diego, California, as our country agonized over this tragedy, there were at least two people who were oblivious to the catastrophic event.

I stood beside my thirty-three-year-old husband of thirteen years as the doctor shut down his life-support system. And in one brief moment, the world became deafeningly silent.

The Lord's hand gently guided me through my misery toward a renewed relationship with Him. I prayed regularly, read my Bible, and learned to trust God to guide me through events and circumstances I couldn't understand. While I was struggling to comprehend the reason for the pain and suffering we experience, He was teaching me to cling to His promise. "For I know the thoughts that I think toward you, saith the Lord, thoughts of peace, and not of evil, to give you an expected end." (Jeremiah 29:11)

A year after Rick's death, I met a man who encouraged me to go to church with him. I realized it was the fellowship of other believers I was missing. As my relationship with God blossomed, so did my relationship with Terry. After four months together we decided to get married. This was a challenge, as my three children all had turbulent emotions connected with someone else taking their dad's place. It was a daunting task to convince them that no one ever takes someone's place, but that there is always room in our hearts to love and be loved by another.

The changes in our family were challenging for all of us, but it seemed that my youngest daughter was having the most difficult time adjusting. We discovered a small Christian school and decided that the intimate environment might benefit Amber both academically and spiritually. It wasn't until her eighth-grade graduation that we understood her new outlook toward her relationship with God and our blended family.

Each of the eight graduating students came to the podium to speak from their hearts to the families gathered to celebrate this momentous day of passage. When it came time for Amber to speak, we realized what a significant event this was for her. The following words were taken from two 6-x-9 inch cards she used for her speech.

Hi, my name is Amber. This is my second year at Mira Mesa Christian. Ever since I've been here God has changed my life extremely. He has shown me that I can love people and trust them. Before I came here, I never really thought too much about God and everything that He does for me. I just wanted to do the things that I wanted to do, even though most of the things I wanted to do were wrong. The time that I really messed up was when I was around 10 years old and my father was really sick, then he died of cancer.

I was mad. I actually hated God. I thought that it was so bad that He took my father away. I just couldn't understand why until my mom met this guy named Terry and she started going to church. Then I started going to church also. And then I figured out that there was a reason that God took my father away. And if I just trusted in God, all things would work out for the best. So I learned to trust God and now I have a wonderful new dad who loves me and cares for me just as if I were his own. Sometimes I get frustrated and I don't understand why things happen to me. Then all I have to do is to go to God and ask Him. Maybe I won't get the answer right then, but eventually everything works out for the best. Like I said, I've changed a lot. But I'm not perfect. And I still do a lot of things wrong, but I do know that in all things God works for the good of those who love him, and we have been called according to His purpose. Thank you for listening and I hope you all have a good night.

In her talk that afternoon, Amber revealed the tremendous transformation that had taken place in our family. But it wasn't until several years later, on Amber's wedding day, that I was aware of how subtly but purposefully our family had bonded.

We spent weeks busily readying ourselves for the grand event. The invitations were mailed, and the beautifully crafted bridal gown and the magnificent cake were worthy of any royal wedding feast. The vows had been exchanged, the covenant sealed, and now my daughter and her husband joined their family and friends for the toast. Before lifting his glass in a toast, Terry reached into his coat pocket and pulled out two considerably faded 6-x-9 inch cards. After Amber's graduation speech, Terry had quietly and purposefully pocketed those cards and tucked them away, confident that on the day of her wedding he would read the words that unveiled God's plan for our family.

As he ushered our daughter into the next season of her life, I tearfully recalled those moments that had validated our hopes and dreams and sealed our family bond years before at that graduation ceremony. I finally understood that in life, even in an uncertain present and an unpredictable future, we can find a glorious and unexpected end. I know now that in a family built on love, there is always room for one more.

Growing a Mustard Seed, Shrinking a Mountain

By Kathryn Heckenbach

If ye have faith as a grain of mustard seed, ye shall say unto this mountain, Remove hence to yonder place; and it shall remove; and nothing shall be impossible unto you.

—MATTHEW 17:20

When I was diagnosed with cancer my mom gave me a necklace that held a tear-shaped piece of glass encasing a single tiny mustard seed. "Remember," she said, as I pulled the necklace out of the box, "this is all the faith you need. God will get you through this." I put the necklace on, and during my three months of chemotherapy and radiation I rarely took it off.

But it made me wonder—what measure do we use for faith? How do we know how much we have? Is it something we are born with? And if so, are we limited to that amount or can we attain more? Is it something we must produce ourselves? There were days during my treatment when I felt that tiny mustard seed represented a colossal and unattainable amount of faith. Ravaged by the chemicals pumped into me each week and the daily radiation treatments, I barely had the strength to stand at times. If I was to be responsible for the production and maintenance of my own faith, then surely I was doomed to fail. The mountain would remain . . . unmovable.

How I wished for the faith I'd seen in others, friends and family members who had suffered tragedies but held fast to God's promises with unwavering belief in His plans for them. My aunt, in particular, had dealt with innumerable health problems for years, but her faithful and obedient heart never faltered. During periods of severe headaches and other daily health struggles, she continued to focus on following God's will. She was always ready with prayer for someone in need, her eyes shining with the knowledge that God would answer perfectly. She exemplified all I yearned to be during my illness.

One day I found myself on the floor, overcome with a wave of depression. The cancer treatments had taken their toll on my body and mind, and I hit a point of desperation. The light at the end of the tunnel, the day I would be declared cancer-free, seemed eons away. The journey was too far, and I no longer had the strength to believe I would make it.

And then I read the apostles' request to Jesus in Luke 17:5, "Increase our faith!" I realized that was what I needed to finish traveling the long and painful road ahead of me—more faith. But where was I to get it? My supply had run dry and I was too weak to produce more on my own. I needed to see my aunt's faith-filled eyes again, and the face that shone with confidence in an ever-present God. But my aunt lived hours away.

With my last ounce of strength I began to pray, reiterating the plea of the apostles. *Dear God, please give me faith. You created me,*

You can add to me. I need that now, more than anything. Please . . . add to my faith . . . increase my faith. With my face pressed against the carpet, and the words barely out of my mouth, I heard the phone ring. I wiped my tear-streaked cheeks as I sat up, and then shakily stood. I reached out and picked up the phone.

"Hello," I answered.

The voice of an angel answered, "Hi, sweetie, this is Aunt B. Are you going to be home for a little while? I'm in town right now and was hoping to stop by."

Suddenly, a mustard seed no longer seemed the size of a mountain.

Broken Window Pains

By Cristy Trandahl

"Mom! I need control!" my three-year-old hollered from his car seat in the back of our Suburban. He wanted the window down on his side of the vehicle but the child safety feature had locked his control button. "Mom, I need control!"

Control. How many times in my own life had I pleaded to God for control? Too many.

In my marriage, how many disagreements (okay, fights) have my husband and I had because we both wanted control over a situation? He wanted to relocate our family to this city. I wanted to live in another town. He wanted to spend our money on this. I wanted to buy that. I wanted our bathroom painted Groovy Golden Yellow, he wanted to paint it . . . Okay, maybe he was right on that one.

In parenting, how many times had I exerted my own will before talking things over with God? I wanted my son and daughters to experience the joy of music, theater, and dance. I enrolled them in Swedish folk dance, children's musicals, and piano lessons . . . but my children are all jocks. They prefer basketball over Bach, soccer over Shakespeare, and fishing over folk dance.

In my job as a writer, how many times have I attempted to control a piece, to make it the story I wanted it to be, instead of allowing the truth of a situation tell its own tale?

As a Christian, how many times have I snowplowed through the liturgy, searching for my own agenda, lamenting: "I didn't get anything out of church!" instead of just being part of the Body of Christ?

We all imagine it would be so easy, so convenient, if, like my boy in the back seat, we could just push that "control" button in life whenever we want to obtain something: Money. Success. Health. A candy bar the size of Rhode Island. We imagine that if everyone did things our way, the world would be a much better place. If only God would conform His will to ours, right?

Then, I think back to the little boy in the backseat . . .

"Mom! I need control!"

"Andrew, honey, the child safety thingy only lets me lower your window from the driver's side. You have to stop pushing your button for mine to work."

My boy just kept pulsing the button with the window icon. "I will make it go down by myself! I need control, Mom!"

Then the window did a funny thing. With me on the driver's seat pushing the control button down and my son in the back seat pushing the control button down, the window went out of whack. After a series of abrupt jolts, the window's movement ceased. It stuck. Jammed. My son and I, passenger and driver, both control commandoes, lost our objective. Because we were unwilling to compromise a little, we both lost a lot of control.

God gave us His Son, the Holy Spirit, the church, and each

other to help us find our way to Him. But sometimes we have to relinquish control over a situation to come to the truth of it. Today, when I am confronted with a new situation—a church teaching, a suffering in the world, a loss, even a success—I try to holler to Christ, up there in the front seat, "Hey, God! I want control of this!" But before I push my own driver's side control I add, "But Your will be done."

It all goes down so much better then.

She Comes from God: Miss Dodie Osteen

By Michael Jordan Segal

I had never met her in person, but I knew about her. In fact, I thought everyone knew about her. And on that bright morning I was finally going to get the opportunity to meet her in person. We were both going to be guests on a local television show discussing the power and importance of prayer in recovery from illness or a traumatic experience.

Dodie Osteen is well known: She is the wife of the late Pastor John Osteen of Houston's huge Lakewood Church, and mother of Pastor Joel Osteen (who followed in his father's footsteps and led the church when his father went to heaven). Miss Dodie, as she likes to be called, was discussing the emotional and physical struggles she had faced when her doctors diagnosed her ailment as liver cancer. I, the son of a rabbi, was discussing the struggle I had faced after being shot in the head and no one, including my surgeon, had given me any hope of survival. Ironically, both "hopeless events" occurred in 1981, but we had never met until that eventful television show decades later.

Off camera, I thanked Dodie for leading the inspiring chapel services every Tuesday in the Memorial Hermann Hospital Chapel.

I work at that hospital helping families and patients overcome illness and injury and "beat the odds." I always attend the chapel service, partly because Dodie's personality and disposition are so warm and inviting. Dodie ministers and encourages everyone in the pews. She is Christian, I am Jewish, but we are *all* God's children.

Over the months of attending the chapel services, I saw many ill children and infants sitting on their parents' laps. Miss Dodie would always pray for them, as well as for anyone else who wished for a personalized prayer. As the weeks passed, we could see many of them improving. I believe Miss Dodie's encouraging and reassuring prayers really helped.

I will never forget the thanks Miss Dodie received from the mother of a child about to be discharged from the hospital. The mother was there in the chapel, as she had been every Tuesday for months during her son's hospitalization. This time she brought her other child with her. Both children were disabled, and the mother shared with Miss Dodie the fact that both children suffered from the same syndrome, a rare genetic disorder with a very high mortality rate. The mother also told Miss Dodie, "Only 600 children who have this ailment are still alive today, and I am blessed to have two of them!" I smiled as the family left the chapel. The reason was simple: the mother's attitude and gratitude, all because of faith.

Miss Dodie Osteen preaches the word of God, and people listen. She is definitely a special person, a person sent from God. I am one of the lucky people who has been blessed to know her, and I thank God for Miss Dodie, as well as for all the other special people who try to help those who are ill and suffering throughout the world.

The Most Unlikely Place

By Kelli Regan

There is no difference, for all have sinned and
fall short of the glory of God,
and are justified freely by his grace through
the redemption that came by Christ Jesus.

—Romans 3:23-24

I stood at the podium and took a deep breath. As I looked out on the sea of expectant faces waiting for me to lead the prayer, my stomach clenched. How in the world did I get here? Terrified to speak in public and the only woman in a room full of men—clearly I didn't belong. But together we sang, clapped with joy, delved into Scripture, shouted "Amen!" and uttered prayers that shook the rafters of heaven. In that place I felt Jesus' love, understood His forgiveness, and marveled at His grace. I could have been in almost any church on any given evening.

But I wasn't in church. I was in a maximum security men's prison. Nothing in my life experience qualified me to be there. Not my nonexistent rap sheet, my culturally sanitized suburban lifestyle, my inexperience with addiction, my college education, my race, and especially not my gender. Yet there I was. In the brightly lit cinderblock room, the ninety congregants looked like a ragtag team of hospital aides. A homogenous mass of light blue, scrub-like shirts and one-size-fits-none black cotton drawstring pants made it hard to tell one inmate from the next. But when I took a closer look I noticed details that revealed each man's individuality. The feet shod in black Chuck Taylor high-tops. The gnarled hands that gripped a tattered Bible. The mouth that mocked and interrupted. The back that slumped. The knees that bent in prayer. And the arms—so many arms—that told stories punctuated by tattoos and scars. Stories of broken homes, abuse, addiction, gangs, and violence. Stories so different from my own. Yet, to my surprise, though I saw faces etched in bitterness, I saw more softened by forgiveness. Eyes I expected to be narrowed in anger instead sparkled with joy. And fists that should by all rights be clenched in rage were opened and lifted in praise.

Two years ago, a small group from my church looked for a way to reach out to the marginalized in society. W tossed around various ideas—homeless shelters, battered women, food kitchens—but none of them stuck. Then someone mentioned prison—an odd suggestion for an upper-middle-class couples' Bible study. Yet, after some thought we unanimously said, "Yes."

Within days we'd made contact with a local prison ministry. Within weeks the ministry's leaders, Bob and Royce, came to our group and shared stories about their work: stories so vivid and inspiring they left us transfixed. Most of us signed on and within months made our debut visit to the urban prison. From the beginning, I decided I'd support the ministry team by quietly praying during the service. Since I never helped lead a worship service and wasn't anxious to start, I figured it was the best I could offer. Besides, doing anything that involved standing in front of an audience or holding a microphone lay solidly outside my comfort zone. *Period.* God knew this. Surely, He'd understand. Each week Bob or Royce asked if anyone had something to share. Each week I shook my head and replied, "Not me." I confirmed my decision with God. *Lord, it's good that I come here. That's enough, isn't it?* I'm not sure He agreed.

After months of watching the services, Bob announced, "Next week you newcomers are going to lead the service." I said, panic-stricken, "We're not ready!" The others didn't agree and accepted the challenge. *Good for them,* I thought. *I just won't participate.* Assignments were divvied up and I remained silent. When only one job remained open, my friend looked at me and asked, "Kelli, can you lead the prayer?"

Cornered, I begrudgingly replied, "Well . . . I'll think about it. I guess if you don't have anyone else. . . ."

For the next seven days my stomach flip-flopped in fear. As I travelled by plane on business that week, I took time to write out my prayer because there was no way I could wing it. Lacking paper, I grabbed the next best thing on an airplane—and probably the most appropriate medium—barf bags. Four of them, to be exact. *Who knows, they just might come in handy.*

Despite my divine pleas that an act of God would keep me from the prison, the dreaded moment arrived. While I felt the heat of nervousness race up my neck and flare across my face, I didn't vomit, faint, or die. In fact, the men responded enthusiastically with shouts of affirmation. And I witnessed the Spirit work far beyond my clumsiness and inelegant words. Instead of feeling embarrassed, I felt honored and humbled.

Bob often says, "Speaking in front of the guys will change you." I think he's right. It would be so easy to enter the correctional facility feeling superior, better than, and more deserving. Certainly my "goodness" sets me apart, doesn't it? I quickly learned the answer is "no." For our goal as Christians isn't *goodness*, it's *Godliness*. By society's standards, these inmates are not good people. But, many are godlier than most people I know on the "outside."

I am in that prison for one reason—because God said, "Go." With each raggedy, passionate, honest worship service I see Him more clearly. When I stand shoulder to shoulder with thieves, rapists, and murderers and we worship together with passion, grace becomes startlingly clear. I know I'm no more deserving of salvation than the inmates. We're all sinners saved by grace. And as I witness men transformed by the truth of the Gospel, it's finally becoming less and less about me and more and more about Him.

How ironic that God showed me the door to my freedom inside the walls of a maximum-security prison. On Tuesday nights, behind soaring barbed-wire walls, Jesus joins us together as one as we offer up our sins. Our brokenness. Our insufficiencies. And because we do—we know the truth. And the truth sets us free.

All Is Well

By Jerry Hendrick

Duduring a Sunday morning worship service in December last year, our pastor asked us to think of our favorite Christmas memory and to share it with whoever was sitting near. I was sitting next to a friend, and both of us briefly shared childhood memories we have of Christmas mornings. We recalled the feelings we had when we woke up, and went to our stockings to see what had been left while we slept. We remembered how magical Christmas mornings felt when we were young. Though the memories I shared with my friend were honest, and probably represent the "happiest" Christmas memories I have, the truth is that I have a much more recent memory that I look back on today as one of my favorites.

In 2006, my daughter Ashley and a few of her friends sang the song "All Is Well" as a part of a special Christmas service at church. On the day the girls sang this song, Ashley was very sick from a recent chemo treatment, and she was experiencing pain and phantom sensations from the amputation of her left leg just two weeks prior. I remember thinking, as I listened to her sing and watched through tear-filled eyes; that all really wasn't well. I remember feeling overwhelmed by what we were going through at the time, and discouraged about the uncertainty of our future.

While the girls sang this song in the hushed and reverent silence of our candle-lit church, my wife, Beth, and sons Aaron, Austin, and I all sat and watched and listened. From our seats near the back, we saw a daughter and sister somehow put aside what she was going through to sing a song of thankfulness for being well. We couldn't believe that Ashley could make it through her song, as all day long she had been lying on our couch; so sick and hurting. She had ridden to church that night with the pink hospital-issued "puke bucket" on her lap, as her stomach was so upset.

While I listened to Ashley sing, everything else that I had been worrying about seemed to fade away, and for a little while at least, I understood our experience in a way I hadn't before. Singing about or making the claim that "all is well" is not meant to be a reference to how you are doing financially or how many presents you expect to give or receive. "All is well" is not a statement that pertains to your current frame of mind or overall outlook on life. It does not regard the selfless acts of compassion you show to strangers near or far, or the money or time you set aside for charity and benevolence. "All is well" is not even intended to speak to the love that you give and receive from close friends or members of your family. And it was apparent that night that the words didn't mean everyone was healthy, either.

To me, the phrase "All is well" is nothing more than a simple reminder that so long as your heart is right with God, everything else will be okay. Wellness, to put it another way, is really only about one thing: our relationship with God. Though I would never want to imply that the other things that I have mentioned don't matter, what really matters most I think is our faith and unwavering commitment to the love and service of our lord, Jesus Christ. When we get that right, everything else tends to take care of itself, and we experience the sense of wellness or peace that this song seems to convey. It's a matter of keeping our focus on God and turning all of the other stressors and demands of life over to Him.

I hope none of us ever forget this most basic yet profound truth: If we love Him, and live our life for Him, then all truly is well.

Miracles Big and Small

A Ministering Spirit

By Judy Lee Green

Are not all angels ministering spirits . . . ?

—Hebrews 1:14

I had been in the hospital for five days and was out of my head with pain and suffering. Though it was mid-afternoon, the curtains were drawn tight. Only a dim light burned in my room. My exhausted husband was asleep in a chair. He did not wake when a nurse came in, shifted me to my left side, and changed the bandages on my incisions.

Rolling to my side caused such intense pain that when she left I did not move. My face was against the bedrail. My right arm was draped through the rail and hanging down toward the floor. *Dear Lord*, I silently prayed, *how much more of this can I stand?*

I was on a morphine pump, nerve desensitizers, muscle relaxants, and injections and pills for pain. I had an IV in each arm, one for meds and fluids and one for blood transfusions, and two drains, one in my back and one in my hip at the site of my incisions. With tears in my eyes I prayed, *Please help the doctors manage this pain. Dear Lord, if it be thy will, allow me some relief so that I can begin to get better and be able to go home.*

Only moments passed, then in the semidarkness of my hospital room a wavering, shapeless, white mist rose off the floor. As I was still on my left side, my face against the bedrail, I saw the mist rise as high as my eyes. I did not move my tortured body but rolled my head back and watched it grow taller. The mist took the shape of a man in a long flowing robe. A loose hood about his head cast a shadow, concealing the features of his face. I felt the gentle touch of a hand on my right shoulder. A soothing voice said to me: "It's all over now." I felt comforted.

"You've had all the pain you can stand." Calm washed over my body.

"Everything's going to be all right." Peace entered my body through His hand. He repeated the same three statements over and over. I fell asleep and slept the rest of the day. A man dressed in nurse's scrubs was standing next to my bed when I woke up. When he told me that he was going to be my night nurse from 7 PM to 7 AM the next morning I was not thrilled. I preferred female nurses. Two surgical incisions, one down my spine and the other across my hip where bone was removed, were not something that I relished sharing with the young man standing by my bed.

"I'm going to lift you," he said, "and move you up in the bed so that you will be more comfortable. I'm not going to hurt you."

He was not a large man and I had my doubts about whether he could move me, but I nodded my head in agreement. He leaned over and told me to put my arms around his neck. As we touched, the smooth skin of his neck brushed against my face. There was no hint of stubble and no smell of harsh cologne or the heavy odor of aftershave. He smelled clean, like rainwater or a summer shower.

I was recovering from a spinal fusion. Prior to the surgery, I could stand for no more than two minutes and could not feel my feet or my legs. I had been in moderate pain for years and severe pain for months. During the surgery, my spine was opened up and donor bone was packed into the open space to keep it from re-closing. A steel rod and screws were inserted to secure and strengthen my spine. Bone had also been taken from my hip and used to stabilize my back.

Almost a week had gone by following the successful surgery, and I was still in extreme pain. And now here was a young night nurse who very quietly and calmly told me that he was going to move me and that he was not going to hurt me. When my husband offered to help, the nurse said that he could do it by himself. I felt calm and trusting when he spoke to me.

With my arms around his neck, he moved me up in bed as gently as if he were moving a newborn baby. It was the least pain that I had felt when being moved. Amazed, I glanced at his name tag for the first time. It simply said *Chris*. Though the other nurses wore the same hard plastic nametags, theirs had both first and last names, R.N. or L.P.N., and their hospital positions imprinted for easy identification. His simply said *Chris*.

He was in and out of my room throughout the night. He brought medication, checked on me frequently, and talked confidently about my recovery in a soothing voice. His presence brought me peace and comfort. As he prepared to leave the next morning I asked him if he would be back at 7:00 PM that night. I had entirely forgotten my bias against male nurses.

"I don't know," he said. "I go wherever I'm needed."

When he left my room I was more comfortable than I had been in the six days since I entered the hospital. One of my surgeons arrived soon after and added additional medication to my drug plan. I felt as though I had turned a corner. When the day nurse came to my room and told me that she would be with me from 7:00 AM to 7:00 PM, I told her how much I liked Chris.

"Chris who?" she said. "I don't know any Chris who works here."

"He only had Chris on his nametag," I told her, "no last name, no position."

After checking with other nurses and the nurse supervisor throughout the morning, I found that none of them had seen him, and no one knew of anyone named Chris who worked on the floor. Some nurses rotate from floor to floor to fill in, I was told, but no one named Chris was on the roster.

"He sounds like an angel," one of them told me. "If he comes back tonight I want to meet him."

"I go wherever I'm needed," he'd said to me. I was better because of him, because of his care. Somehow, I knew that I would not see him again.

Healing Through Spiritual Saturation

By Diana M. Amadeo

The radiologist had to be kidding. I had been having mammograms faithfully for years with negative readings. This time, though, he told me there was a suspicious area on the right side. Curiously, it was exactly where a pin-point of stabbing pain had been plaguing me the past six months. Doctors had dismissed it as a side effect of multiple sclerosis (MS). Because multiple sclerosis can cause random neuropathy pain, I had accepted this like everything else I had to accept with MS. But now I was faced with possible breast cancer. My spiritual passiveness and acceptance were provoked. I was angry.

The surgeon viewed the mammogram and elected to wait six months to repeat the film before doing a biopsy. I was devastated. Six months for cancer cells to multiply? Biopsy now, please, so I don't have to live with this anxiety. But the answer was no, there was a good possibility the lesion was benign. Funny, I always thought a negative biopsy was a good thing. Now it was labeled an unnecessary procedure.

So I waited. But I had an overpowering feeling that I couldn't be passive. Because I was a former registered nurse, I knew very well how to research and institute changes into my lifestyle for optimum health. Latest research suggests a low-fat, low-carbohydrate diet plus adding flax and soy to daily intake may reduce the proliferation of cancer cells. Exercise is a strong component to health. Psychologically, a determined and positive attitude is conducive to maintaining good health. Emotionally, a good support system is essential. And study after study emphasizes the power of prayer and a strong spiritual life as essential in holistic healing.

I have long been an advocate of "centering prayer" meditation. The rhythmic inhalation and exhalation while focusing on God and detaching from the world has brought me profound peace especially in turbulent times. During this period of my life, meditation took on a special purpose—the spiritual release of all that was toxic within (guilt, fear, anger, depression) and the filling within me of God's love, peace, and joy.

I have dealt with the devastating effects of multiple sclerosis for years. But this situation needed to be handled differently. The tactics had changed. I called my parents.

My mother, a devout Christian, immediately put me on her congregation's prayer line. My ten siblings, spread out across the country, did the same. I contacted every person in my e-mail address book and asked for prayers. Everyone responded. I was put on local prayer books of intentions and many prayer lines at great distance. I attended healing services, experienced hands-on healing and anointings. I continued with prayer and religious meetings and my service to those homebound. I would only put positive things into my mind, body, and soul. Crime, war, and injustice were viewed with detachment. I believe that energy follows thought, so God, family, love, prayer, and blessings were moved to the forefront where they belonged.

My centered prayer or meditative sessions began to evolve into sweet nothingness. I basked in the silence. It felt as if this special communion with God was washing away my infirmities. That pinpoint shooting nerve pain from my right breast was gone. Even my MS symptoms seemed to lessen in severity.

At the six-month recheck mammogram there was no change. The surgeon was very positive, citing that this may just be a "new normal" variation for me. He would order another mammogram in six months to check my progress. This time, instead of challenging him, I agreed. In my heart, I felt all was well. He remarked how my disposition had changed from intense fear to confidence. And something else—I looked radiant and happy. In amazement, I showed him how, for the first time in ten years, I could ambulate by cane instead of crutches or the use of a power chair. He asked what was happening. My only guess was spiritual saturation. I was being flooded by love.

As saints have long known, love blurs the distinction between persons. Forgiveness comes more easily. Grudges, anger, and fear can be quietly transformed to compassion. Love allows letting go of past problems, sadness, or any negative act we cling to out of fear. Acts of kindness may follow. Love has powerful side effects. Love heals. In this fast-paced world where the weak are left behind and the strong seem to prosper—spiritual, emotional, psychological, and physical strengths require balance.

Throughout the Gospels, Jesus cured the blind, the crippled, and those possessed with the words, "Your faith has healed you."

He planted the seed of wellness with the understanding that his loving healing must be nurtured in order to reach full fruition. We must respect his work and do our best to maintain it.

On the one-year anniversary of my abnormal mammogram, I walked in unaided to have a repeat film done. The tech and radiologist were astounded at the benign status of my MS. A few days later, I received by mail the information that my mammogram was also benign. All traces of enlarged lymph nodes and density were gone.

Could this all be coincidence, fate, or a normal progression of the human condition? Or is spiritual saturation a catalyst for the healing and rejuvenation of mind, body and spirit? Is this all just a temporary remission of the inevitable consequences of a chronic and perhaps more serious disease? As my primary physician advises, "Don't doubt, don't question your recovery. Keep doing whatever you are doing. And enjoy your newfound life."

The Year Santa Got a Divorce

By Pam Bostwick

"I don't want to have Christmas anyway," hollered my son Jason, as he threw down a box of ornaments. Fragments scattered all over the floor while his brother Jeremy watched in sullen silence.

Jason stormed from the room. "Daddy is Santa Claus and he's getting a divorce!" I heard his door slam.

"That was dumb," Jeremy complained as he started picking up pieces of glass. The shattered decorations reminded me of the boys' broken lives since their dad had gone.

My throat tightened with emotion and I tried to pray. *Oh God, where are you?* I felt no calming peace. Through tear-filled eyes I looked up to see the star atop the tree mocking me with its cheerful facade. Under the evergreen's sparse branches, there were no presents. The number of gifts I had to give each boy could be counted on one hand. On my limited income, I'd managed to buy a few name-brand clothing items at Goodwill, I'd collected baseball cards, and baked some homemade goodies. Despair overwhelmed me. Santa Claus and my husband's "Ho! Ho! Ho!" wouldn't stop at our house this year.

A loud knock startled me. Jeremy went to answer and I wiped my eyes. "Who could that be?"

Jeremy peeked through the peephole, shouted "Mom!" as he flung the door open wide, and then ran outside. I followed in anticipation.

I looked over his shoulder and gasped in awe when I saw two brand-new bicycles on the porch. Jeremy touched the silver chrome handlebars shining in the moonlight. "Is that for me?"

Who knew my boys longed for bikes I couldn't afford? I wondered. With trembling hands, I grasped the note hanging from the seat.

All at once the yard flooded with light. "What's going on?" Jason called as he tore past me. His eyes were as big as silver dollars. "Wow!" he shouted as he jumped on the other bike.

I could hardly read the note through my tears. "We feel Jason and Jeremy must be having it hard right now. Let them know they're loved. We're praying for all of you."

Santa had come in the form of someone who cared enough to sense my children's sadness. A person chose not to judge that sometimes divorce has to be.

Jeremy grabbed me in a bear hug. "I love my bike."

Jason punched the air. "I really like mine too." He gave me a sheepish look. "I'm sorry about the broken ornaments, Mom. I'll clean it up."

I glanced up at the twinkling stars. "I wish all families could be blessed like we are this year," I breathed.

We all became quiet until Jeremy offered, "I've got some Legos I could give the orphans."

"Me too," Jason chimed in. "It *is* Jesus's birthday, the best time to give stuff away."

"That's really nice of you boys to think of less fortunate kids."

"Why not?" Jason shrugged. "Jesus has sure shown how much he loves us."

"Those poor kids don't have anything or anyone," Jeremy reflected. "We're lucky to have you, Mom."

I smiled. My heart overflowed with God's love. Jason and Jeremy were experiencing the Christmas spirit because another had been willing to share the season's joy, selflessly giving not just one but two bicycles. God had answered my prayers.

More Precious than Gold

By Patricia Taylor

I was very young when my mother passed a wonderful gift on to me, saying, "Here is the proof God exists. He is the way, the truth, and the life." These words have lingered with me throughout my life.

It was a cold and wintry day in 1920. My mother was young and lived at home in St. Paul, Minnesota, with her parents. That day she wore an apron like her mother as they worked in the kitchen together. As they fixed lunch, the doorbell rang. My mother was expecting a friend and her little daughter. She was happy to see them and invited them in out of the cold, snowy weather. Before having them take their coats off, she insisted on taking pictures with her new camera. It was then the latest invention in photography, and everyone was excited about taking pictures.

Mother knew her friend's little girl wasn't well, and this would be a good time to get some pictures of her. The pretty little girl had big brown eyes and auburn hair that lay on her shoulders. She was dressed in a brown heavy woolen coat and wore a snug fur cap on her head. Muffs kept her hands warm, and her feet were covered with high-laced boots. Mother and her friend took the little girl outside and they all stood on my grandmother's back porch. It was a perfect spot to take pictures. A light snow that had fallen the night before glistened in the morning sun. The child posed while the camera clicked. Suddenly, my mother's apron strings caught on her camera, and it wouldn't work anymore. The two ladies felt sure they had taken enough pictures that morning and would not be disappointed when the developed photos came back.

In those days, the camera with the film inside had to be sent to Rochester, New York, to the Kodak factory, and it was several months before the camera and developed photos were returned. In the meantime, the little girl passed away from an unknown illness.

When the package of pictures arrived, my mother and grandmother quickly opened it. They were eager to see the photographs of the darling little girl. At least my mother's best friend would have these memories of her little daughter! But to everyone's disappointment, not one picture of the little girl standing on my grandmother's back porch had turned out. But then something else appeared. Underneath the pile of blank pictures, a glossy black and white picture showed through. To Mother's and Grandmother's amazement, it was a picture of Jesus Christ standing in the fresh-fallen snow beside my grandmother's lilac bush. Jesus' right hand was raised in the sign of peace.

God came in this picture himself, giving assurance to the mother of the little girl that she would always be with Him. Mother quoted Scripture, "I am the way, the truth, and the life:

no man cometh unto the Father, but by me (John 14:6)."

I never tired of asking about the picture that my mother carried in her wallet. I would ask, "Who is that man? Why is he standing in the snow?" As I grew a little older, I could hardly wait each year for summer vacation and our annual trip to my grandmother's house in Minnesota. There I would stand and marvel at the spot where Jesus had stood beside the lilac bushes in my grandmother's backyard.

Like Lazarus

By Kathryn Heckenbach

I was twelve when I made the decision to accept Christ, but within two years my life seemed to fall apart. My parents divorced, leaving me full of anger and mistrust. I started dating an older boy, the first of a long string of failed relationships. Rather than treating my body like a temple, as the Bible instructs (1 Corinthians 6:19-20), I abused my body by consuming alcohol and drugs, bouncing between junk food and starvation diets, and partying night after night.

I still considered myself a Christian, however. There was no doubt in my mind that Christ was the Son of God, sent to deliver me from my sins. I just felt too angry to let go of those sins, and I was getting away with so much without consequence. Or so I thought.

As the years passed, I began to take steps in the right direction. My life leveled out, and I began to thank God for protecting me during my reckless years. I married a wonderful man and eventually had two beautiful children. But something was still missing. I finally began to notice the Holy Spirit's daily nudges, and told my husband I felt it was time for me to return to church.

As a family, we found a church that became a home for us, and I announced my wish to recommit my life to Christ.

And then came my diagnosis: stage 1B adenocarcinoma of the cervix. I was devastated, of course, because I feared dying. But more than that, I felt betrayed. I had spent years living selfishly and had no health problems. When I finally decided to return to the arms of my loving God, I was diagnosed with a life-threatening illness. *It's not fair!* I cried to God. *I've done what You asked! I've come back, and this is how You welcome me?*

Despite my confusion and anger, I knew I needed to rely on God to bring me through this ordeal. I pushed aside my negative emotions and turned to Him for comfort, cried out to Him in despair, prayed daily for healing, and said over and over, *Please, God, I want to love You with all my heart and soul . . . build my faith and help me love You.*

And He did. He worked through family and friends, church members, nurses and doctors, and the prayers sent to Him from people I had never even met. He didn't heal me immediately as I had requested, but after three months of treatment I was proclaimed cancer-free.

I soon began to ponder the reasons God could have had for not healing me sooner. Why make me go through all of that? I had already decided to trust in Him, and He could have easily zapped the tumor away. And then I read the story of Lazarus found in John 11:1-44. Jesus could have healed Lazarus immediately, but He chose to wait. Healing Lazarus from an illness would have been wonderful, but would not have shown the full glory of God. How much more magnificent to raise a man from the dead after days of entombment! God's hand could not be denied, or ignored, or written off in that circumstance.

The same could be said for my situation. The tumor inside me had started years before, as a minor genetic change in a cell. It took time for that change to spread, all the while seeming to me as though my life choices made no difference. Had God healed me immediately after returning to Him I would never have known the tumor had ever been there, and thus never known He had performed such a miracle. Had He healed me soon after the onset of symptoms or diagnosis, it would have been written off as inaccurate lab results, a hormonal imbalance that had corrected itself, or an anomaly of our amazing human body and its ability to heal.

God did not want those things to happen, though. He wanted me to see that His presence had undeniably made the difference. Everything had been perfectly orchestrated by Him. My type of cervical cancer is often not found until later stages because it is not easily detected, yet my symptoms started in stage 1 due to an abnormal growth spurt of the tumor. My treatment centers were located minutes from my husband's office, and he was by my side every time I needed him. I had more help with the kids than I could have ever hoped for, with grandparents and friends tending their every need. Even the song that played the first time I lay down on the radiation table was a gift from God—"I Can Only Imagine" by MercyMe began the second the technician left me alone in the room. The song is about a person trying to imagine what he will do when he comes face-to-face with God at the end of his life.

One of my nurses once told me that my chemotherapy regime was designed to bring me "as close to death as possible, and then back again." She, of course, was referring to my body and giving credit to the doctors and their medical advances. But I know the truth: God was in control the entire time, bringing about what no human can accomplish alone—my spiritual healing. I was emotionally entombed for years, and He brought me back through a display of His power that will never let me stray from Him again.

Little Cherubs
and Teens

Introducing a
Little Religion

By Kathy Fitzgerald

The Sunday school teacher told a story about Jesus and drew a large picture of the cross on a flip chart. The children were given blank sheets of paper and instructed to draw and color their own crosses. As my daughter shouted enthusiastically, "Oh Mommy, do I get to color the big X, too?" I thought, *Hmmm . . . maybe this kid could use a bit more religion.*

I thought we had done a fair job of introducing religion to our daughter's life. Occasionally we read the "Jesus" books (aka the children's Bibles received at her baptism). She knew about God. She knew what a prayer was. When we thought it was time to get serious about church, we started attending regularly and I took her to the children's liturgy program during Mass at our local parish. And she learned a bit more about the "big X."

I thought we were on the right track until a few months later. One Sunday we joined my husband's Irish Catholic family for dinner, and as is customary at such events, we said grace together before eating. This is something my daughter, for reasons I do not quite understand, abhors. She put her hands over her ears and had a sour look on her face during the entire blessing. When we were finished, she sat back in her chair and said loudly, "Well, I'm glad we don't do that at *our* house!" Lots of discreet and amused smiles appeared around the table. This was cute enough coming from a five-year-old, but I still felt obligated to state, "For the record, we *do* try sometimes!"

Now, as part of our efforts to firm up commitment to church, set a good example, and introduce a bit more religion, I volunteer for the children's liturgy program. It is the easiest volunteer gig in the world. Once a month I take the children for the first half of Mass, read them a Coles Notes' version of that day's Gospel, engage them with a few easy questions, and hand out the coloring sheets. As I was preparing for my monthly stint at children's liturgy recently, I found there was no one in the office to give me the code to the photocopier. How was I going to get the coloring sheets prepared for the kids? What would happen? Would they revolt? Would I face mutiny in the children's room? Would I be "unvolunteered"? But then I remembered the day my daughter wanted to color the "big X." *No problem*, I assured myself, *I can handle this. I have been leading this program once a month for five months now; I am a seasoned deliverer of religious education for children ages four to eight. Bring it!*

So I read the Gospel to the kids. Our story was about the twelve apostles and included a brief bio on each. I decided to wing it with the following: "So, boys and girls, the apostles were all very *different* people who came together to make great things happen. Just like each one of us are all *different*. Just like in your classroom or on your soccer team. *Different* people coming together from *different* backgrounds with *different* skills work together to make things happen. Just like Jesus did with the apostles."

I smiled proudly. I was so pleased with myself. *Excellent work using the Gospel to celebrate diversity,* I thought to myself, *just excellent.* "So what I would like you to do today, children," I continued, "is each take a blank sheet of paper and draw the twelve apostles. And draw them each *differently.*"

I am so on my game, I thought excitedly, *this even includes counting—so educational!* I didn't stop to think that pride is considered a sin in some circles. I walked around the room, surveying my brilliant lesson plan in action. I noticed, not surprisingly, that my own daughter was drawing fairies. Another little girl proudly showed me the large pumpkin she drew. As she turned her paper over she told me that she was now drawing a ghost. The Holy Ghost? I felt my confidence waning.

With a few minutes left, I told the children it was time to start finishing up and putting away the crayons. A little boy excitedly approached me and pushed his work in my face. *How eager to please they are at this age,* I thought.

"This is how Jesus would look dressed in a Spiderman costume!"

I smiled, feeling slightly defeated, and also slightly comforted by the knowledge that we were not the only family trying to introduce a little religion.

Do Turkeys Really Wear Striped Socks

By Annmarie B. Tait

I t's pretty safe to say that I've never come face-to-face with a live turkey. Oh, I may have passed a truckload of them on the highway somewhere, just never close enough for wardrobe inspection. However, while teaching Sunday school I discovered quite by accident that most of the first-graders in my class were well acquainted with turkeys. Especially when it came to the hosiery they wore.

The whole thing started with an art project we worked on the Sunday before Thanksgiving. After I passed out plain white paper to the class, each child traced his or her own hand on the sheet of paper with instructions to color it in to look like a turkey. As a kid without enough talent to draw a recognizable stick figure, I usually dreaded art class. That's why I loved the idea of this assignment. Even the least talented children could trace their own hands, draw a face on the thumb, and turn the remaining fingers into colorful feathers. I had high hopes the class would enjoy it but never once did I suspect that at the end of the day the person who would enjoy it and learn the most from it was me.

As the children colored in their turkeys, I walked around the room and asked each boy and girl to tell us all three things for which they were thankful. The children overflowed with reasons to give thanks. I heard everything from "I'm thankful for my little brother," to "I'm thankful Grandma doesn't pinch my cheeks anymore." Humorous or not, each reason to give thanks was expressed with the innocence and sincerity that thrives in the heart of a six-year-old child.

At the end of class I collected the turkeys to hang on the church bulletin board, but accidentally placed them in my tote bag with my book of children's Bible stories. Later that evening as I was getting organized for the start of the work week, I picked up my tote bag and discovered the treasure chest of priceless art. Yes indeed, that year my class turned out an astonishing flock of turkeys. The art project proved to me without a doubt that somewhere along the line these kids encountered a turkey (or perhaps several) that had a hankering for hosiery. I know it sounds crazy but it had to be true. Why else would more than three-quarters of the class draw turkeys sporting socks? From what I could see, none of these kids thought it unusual for a turkey to wear socks. They did not call specific attention to it with arrows or stick figures pointing or anything like that. And what I found most peculiar of all is that none of these turkeys wore *solid-colored* socks. Every single feathered pair of potential drumsticks that paraded across the page was decked out in *multicolored striped* socks.

Well, by now I was belly-laughing in a big way. With tears of laughter rolling down my cheeks, I stood in my kitchen and looked up to the heavens. *So what's the deal, Lord?* I thought. *Do turkeys wear socks or what?* It seemed a strange phenomenon to me. I mean none of them had shoes on, only socks. It just is not *normal*. Or is it? What is normal? I thought about it for a moment. Is *normal* the label I apply only to things and situations that meet my approval? Ahhh . . . at last the light bulb moment had arrived. Right then and there I accepted the challenge of letting go of this narrow-minded view once and for all in my life. I cast my eyes toward heaven yet again, but this time I yelled "uncle."

"Normal is as you would have it Lord, not as I deem appropriate. Is that right? Do I have it now?" I waited for an answer but no rolling thunder or bellowing voices broke the silence. Somewhat disappointed, I looked down at the kitchen table. Assembled before me was one hilarious flock of knock-kneed turkeys festooned in a color wheel of neon-striped leg warmers. Without uttering one single gobble, the message came through loud and clear.

Then and there I resolved never to place a level of expectation between me and any child ever again. Instead, I set my sights on praising their efforts and supporting their willingness to try, no matter what the outcome. I asked God to give me patience and understanding along with an appetite to embrace with gusto the idea that *normal* is as God has created it; exclusive to every child and situation. But mostly, I thanked God for the gift of these wonderful children and for their collective ability to help me refocus and channel my effort to a more positive end.

For all I know, turkeys really do wear striped socks. Maybe by next Thanksgiving they'll be wearing sneakers, too. I can hardly wait to find out.

That Abby Would Have a Big Bunk Bed, Too

By Shaundra Taylor

I stumbled into a moment of sweetness tonight so pure, so tender, it took my breath away.

It was made all the more remarkable by the contrast of the minutes before. I was on my own with the kids tonight, and as I herded
them upstairs for bedtime, they both managed to earn timeouts in
the loud, irritating, *Let's-take-our-frustration-with-the-day-out-on-
Mommy* kind of way. Once I had them both in their rooms for a
little cool-down time, I hopped on the computer to check my e-
mail, wondering just how long the next twenty minutes would be.

Fortunately, the few minutes of alone time seemed to settle us
all down, and the pajama and tooth-brushing routine carried on
uneventfully. My agreement with my son, Ben, is that we'll have
time to read books if he's ready for bed by the time I'm done putting Abby down. This time, he was ready before I even started
reading books with Abby, so he grabbed his Teddy and blankie
and joined us in the oversized green rocking chair in Abby's room.
Thus began a few moments of parental bliss.

As we read, Abby was sandwiched between me and Ben, and
the air was filled with alternating giggles, exclamations, and small

gestures of affection. When we finished the books, I turned off the light and asked who wanted to pray and sing.

Ben said he did, and so he prayed, beginning with our customary prayer, "Now I Lay Me Down to Sleep," which led into "Dear Jesus . . . " He thanked God for all of our family, immediate and extended, for our yummy dinner earlier, for Abby again, and then prayed that Abby would have a big bunk bed, too. This must be the ultimate request for a four-year-old who adores his own bunk bed, and I was moved by his generosity toward his sister.

Then he began to sing, and the room grew quiet except for his strong, confident voice, which, though lacking pitch, did not lack soul. The three of us rocked in that green chair, content to share those precious, snuggly, end-of-the-day moments together as Ben sang. At one point, Abby crawled onto my lap and laid her head down on my shoulder, perfectly stilled by Ben's music. My eyes grew moist with gratitude.

When he finished singing, they exchanged precious "Night nights" in their little voices and snuggled a minute together in the chair, their arms wrapped gently around each other, happy to stay there indefinitely. They adore each other—they really do. In each other's eyes, they are the sun, moon, and stars. I let them snuggle for longer than I normally would, reveling in their love for each other.

When I finally lifted Abby into my arms to carry her to her crib and Ben walked to the door, they both started singing "You Are My Sunshine" again, independent of each other. Ben continued singing into his room; Abby sang in the endearing way only a baby on the brink of girlhood can—in round, soft words, rising and falling with the melody of the song, some syllables indistinguishable from the next. I kissed her, laid her down, and quietly closed the door behind me.

Few things fill my heart like their genuine affection for each other, and tonight, it overflowed. When I see them in these moments of pure love, I get a glimpse of what I think God must feel, and desire, for His children. There's a reason that all of His commandments—all of Scripture, really—can be summed up by the simple yet profound command to "Love your neighbor." When I see Ben and Abby enjoying each other so completely, loving each other so unselfishly, with no regard for themselves, my joy is unspeakable. Everything is as it should be. It is the fulfillment of every hope I would have for them.

It is what God the Father must long for from us: to put away our agendas, our religion, our politics, and our fear of losing our toys, to actually see, know, and love each other. To pray that we'll all have bunk beds, not in spite of our differences, but because through our differences, we can actually know Him more fully, more completely.

I stumbled into a holy night tonight. And it was very good.

A Different Jonah Story

By Mimi Greenwood Knight

You're probably familiar with the first Jonah story. Well, this one's a bit different. It begins in the Bible, yes, but not in the book of Genesis. Rather, my Jonah tale originated in Psalms— Psalms 37:4, to be exact—which promises, "Delight yourself in the Lord and He will give you the desires of your heart."

I first read that verse early one morning as I stole a little quiet time away from my three kids and husband. I thought, *Cool! If I want something, God will give it to me.* But as I spent time meditating on it, I realized it wasn't the things I desire that God was promising to give me. It was the desires themselves. God is promising that, if I delight in Him, He will cause me to want the things He wants for me. That's even better!

I decided to pray that verse as an open invitation to God. For thirty days I prayed, *Lord, whatever this desire is,* (I felt strongly that there was something) *I invite you to place it on my heart. Cause me to want what You want for me more than I've ever wanted anything before.* Well, His ways are not our ways and God answered my prayer, not by causing me to want something, but by showing me how much He'd already given me.

Suddenly I saw my life like an outsider looking in. My husband, David, and I have three bright, beautiful, happy, healthy children. We live in a safe community with excellent public schools, belong to a loving church family, have a beautiful home in the country, supportive extended families, great neighbors, and we both work at jobs we like. My proverbial cup runneth over.

I was working on an article at the time about families paying for college. I'd gone to great lengths to find families to interview from around the country in a mix of socioeconomic situations. As I contacted them I was surprised to realize that they all had one thing in common. Without exception they'd adopted some or all of their children. *Weird coincidence*, I thought. I asked a few questions about their adoptions, just to be polite. But I didn't need the information for my article so I soon forgot it. At least I tried to. That's when a funny thing happened.

I started seeing adoption everywhere I looked. In the grocery store, I'd spot a blond-haired couple with an Asian baby, then I'd turn the corner and see another. I'd run into old friends who'd tell me all about their adoptions. People I'd known for years would say out of the blue, "Well, you know I'm adopted." (I didn't.) I'd turn on the radio to a program about adoption. Turn on the TV—adoption again. When God decides to put something in front of your face, He is far from subtle. How in the world was I going to tell my fifty-three-year-old husband that I was pretty sure God wanted us to adopt?

I confided in my friend, Paula, a beautiful Christian whose opinion I value. She said, "Mimi, God is not in the business of breaking up marriages. Do you really think He would put this on

READER/CUSTOMER CARE SURVEY

UHFG

We care about your opinions! Please take a moment to fill out our online Reader Survey at **http://survey.hcibooks.com.**

As a **"THANK YOU"** you will receive a **VALUABLE INSTANT COUPON** towards future book purchases

as well as a **SPECIAL GIFT** available only online! Or, you may mail this card back to us.

| First Name | | MI. | | Last Name | |

| Address | | | | City | |

| State | | Zip | | Email | |

1. Gender
- ☐ Female
- ☐ Male

2. Age
- ☐ 8 or younger
- ☐ 9-12
- ☐ 13-16
- ☐ 17-20
- ☐ 21-30
- ☐ 31+

3. Did you receive this book as a gift?
- ☐ Yes
- ☐ No

4. Annual Household Income
- ☐ under $25,000
- ☐ $25,000 - $34,999
- ☐ $35,000 - $49,999
- ☐ $50,000 - $74,999
- ☐ over $75,000

5. What are the ages of the children living in your house?
- ☐ 0 - 14
- ☐ 15+

6. Marital Status
- ☐ Single
- ☐ Married
- ☐ Divorced
- ☐ Widowed

7. How did you find out about the book?
(please choose one)
- ☐ Recommendation
- ☐ Store Display
- ☐ Online
- ☐ Catalog/Mailing
- ☐ Interview/Review

8. Where do you usually buy books?
(please choose one)
- ☐ Bookstore
- ☐ Online
- ☐ Book Club/Mail Order
- ☐ Price Club (Sam's Club, Costco's, etc.)
- ☐ Retail Store (Target, Wal-Mart, etc.)

9. What attracts you most to a book?
(please choose one)
- ☐ Title
- ☐ Cover Design
- ☐ Author
- ☐ Content

10. What subject do you enjoy reading about the most?
(please choose one)
- ☐ Parenting/Family
- ☐ Relationships
- ☐ Recovery/Addictions
- ☐ Health/Nutrition
- ☐ Christianity
- ☐ Spirituality/Inspiration
- ☐ Business Self-help
- ☐ Women's Issues
- ☐ Sports
- ☐ Pets

Comments

The ULTIMATE Series

your heart so heavily and not put it on David's too?" It made sense
but I was still scared.

I'd been e-mailing one of the moms from my article, asking
questions about their overseas adoption. I started printing out her
e-mails and casually leaving them in the exact spot where David
drinks his morning coffee, hoping he'd read them. Finally, I mus-
tered the courage to ask him if he'd noticed any of the messages.
He said he had and he loved the idea. I swallowed hard, asked,
"Do you think we ought to do that?"—and held my breath.

"No. Why should we spend $40,000 to adopt overseas when
we could put $40,000 in a college fund and adopt from this coun-
try?" I couldn't believe my ears. David had lost his mind too!

That night we sat the kids down and told them what we were
considering. They went ballistic. They wanted a baby. And they
wanted one *now*! We explained that we'd have to wait until a
baby became available. It felt good to finally give in to what God
wanted, but in truth I was scared to death.

Surely God was overestimating me. I was forty-three years old.
I was already balancing a lot with three kids. What if the child
came with emotional issues? I wasn't trained to handle that.
Maybe God had selected a physically or mentally challenged
child for us. What did I know about caring for a special needs
baby? And I already worried about that inevitable day when he
might want to meet his birth parents.

We began praying for our baby every morning. Not knowing if he
was born yet or if his mother was pregnant with him, we prayed for him
and for her and for everyone involved in caring for our baby-to-be. We
prayed that we'd know how to be the best family possible for him.

Fast forward five months. I received a call from an adoption worker who said, "We have a one-year-old boy entering the system. Do you want him?" *Do we want him?* My knees buckled. *Do we want him?* What kind of question is that?

"Yes, yes, we want him!"

That was one of the strangest phone calls I've ever received. *Someone is calling to offer me a human being,* I thought. *How surreal is this?* But for the moment all my doubts were dormant. This is what God wanted and He's bringing it to pass. *He loves me so much.*

"But we don't have a car seat, diapers, clothes, or bottles," I panicked. Not knowing the age of the baby we'd get had made it impossible to prepare like we wanted to. We had a crib and high chair—that was it.

"No problem. We'll have the case worker meet you at Walmart. You can get everything you need there. Tomorrow. Four o'clock. Okay?" My knees were mush. My mind was numb. I hung up without asking the baby's name or hair color or anything.

At the designated time, David was stuck in a meeting so the kids and I made a frantic dash for Walmart, camera in tow, to the diaper aisle where we'd agreed to meet. No one was there. We stood watching every cart that passed. One woman passed with a baby dressed in pink, another with a baby too old, another too young. Finally a woman looked at us and waved. In her cart was a tiny boy dressed in camouflage pants and a muscle shirt. He smiled right away and when I reached for him, he leapt into my arms.

We brought him home and spent the evening in amazement, watching everything he did. Then we spent half the night watching him sleep. I remembered a scripture which I now call my

Jonah verse. It's Ephesians 3:20, which reminds us that God is able to do exceedingly abundantly above all that we ask or think. Ain't it the truth?

That Sunday we went up in front of our church family and presented our new son. We asked everyone to pray that we could be the family Jonah needs. The church threw a baby shower and gave us everything we needed and then some. That was four years ago. Jonah has grown into a lively, delightful kindergartener who never met a bug, a frog, a puddle, or a tractor he doesn't love. We wonder daily what our lives would be like without him. Two months ago, he asked me to explain again how he could invite Jesus into his heart. That Sunday, our church family offered praise and thanksgiving as we watched him "stir the baptismal waters." He even told us that night when the sunset was particularly spectacular, "Hey, look! I think God did that because He's proud of me for inviting Jesus into my heart and getting bath-a-tized."

The next morning he was engaging in his favorite pastime—climbing way too high in a tree and scaring his mother half to death. I shouted, "Oh, look at that cute little squirrel climbing Mommy's magnolia tree."

"No, Mom," he said in his silliest voice. "I'm not a squirrel. I'm your little gift from God. Remember?"

I suppose that says it all.

Stealing from Jesus

By Benjamin Snow

I felt guilty. But I wanted the ice cream, and I wanted the candy, and I wanted Ralph to like me. And more than all of that, I wanted to not get caught. I slid the quarter across the counter as I had for the past several Sunday mornings, and I accepted my hot fudge sundae in return. It was not a fair trade—my soul for a few ounces of sweetened, frozen milk. The money was stolen and, to make it an even bigger sin, I'd stolen it from Jesus himself. I was so worried about offending God and Jesus—not to mention that I was terrified of my mother finding out—that somehow the ice cream didn't taste very good.

I was eight years old. I'd recently moved to a new town, and Ralph was the only friend I had. In fact, there had been many recent changes in my life. My parents had divorced and my mother had dragged me and my four year-old sister, Katie, back to Pennsylvania from the only home we'd known in sunny southern California. Then, just as we were settling in to our new lives, she remarried and moved us again. It was only a thirty-mile distance, but to me it seemed like a different universe. In less than two years, I'd gone from a trailer park in

Long Beach to my grandparents' suburban Pittsburgh home to a small Mayberry-like western Pennsylvania town. I'd attended three schools in two grades, and I felt very much alone.

To the chagrin of my jealous little sister, I "got" to attend catechism every Saturday morning in our new parish. My mother was a devout Catholic, and we never missed a Sunday service, either. Her new husband was a lapsed Catholic, and he had no interest in attending with us. My mother would walk Katie and me from our house to Mass every Sunday. She was pregnant with my second sister, Alice, and making the walk became more difficult for her with every passing week. She was a small woman and Alice was a big baby. By the time school let out for the summer, Mom was so big (and uncomfortable) that she could no longer walk to church. I didn't mind at all; I thought I'd get the summer off, but my mother was determined that I'd get my spiritual guidance without her.

After Mass one Sunday, my mother talked to Father Brian about her expected absences from services, and plans for the soon-to-be-born baby's baptism. Father Brian asked who would be bringing Katie and me to Mass when my mother had to stay home. Mom told him that there was no one available, that she was afraid that we'd have to miss services as well.

"Benny is a big boy now, Mrs. Snow. He can walk by himself," was the priest's simple solution.

Mom was uncertain, but then Father Brian sealed the deal by reminding her that I was already walking to catechism by myself every Saturday. "Don't worry," he assured her, "we'll keep a special eye on him."

And thus my fate was sealed. I'd have to go to Mass every Sunday morning while my snotty little sister got to stay home and play with friends. After trying to figure out every possible way I could change my fate, I finally gave up, and resigned myself to being a good Catholic boy.

But fate, in the form of Ralph, intervened. Ralph was a rough-and-tumble kid who lived on top of the hill above the church. I'd seen him at school, but it was at catechism where we became friends. At Holy Family Church, catechism was held in a small room in the basement. The only window, at the top of the wall just under the ceiling, was at street level. The room was oppressively hot, and the nun was oppressively strict. I hated going to catechism. There are too many fun things for eight-year-old boys to do on summer Saturday mornings. Being glowered at by a cranky nun didn't even begin make it onto my list of fun things to do over summer vacation. And it turned out that I had a kindred spirit in Ralph.

Like me, Ralph was a smart-alecky, fun-loving boy. Neither of us could sit still during the instruction, and the exasperated nun was always sending us to Father Brian to be "straightened out." For an eight-year-old boy, being sent to the priest was as frightening as being sent to the principal's office in regular school. She may as well have threatened us with the penitentiary. We heeded the threats at first, but after repeated warnings resulted in no punishment, we began to ignore them. Eventually though, Sister Catherine tired of our shenanigans and sent us to the priest. It turned out that we didn't have to fear Father Brian. The kindly priest was gentle with us, and instead of punishing us, he tried to appeal to our better natures. He didn't yell at us, or threaten us, or punish as good Sister did. Father Brian didn't use a ruler, and he didn't make us write an apology hundreds of times. He spoke to us kindly about responsibility, and manners, and polite behavior. He was sympathetic. After all, he'd been an eight-year-old boy one summer, too!

He kept us in line for a while, but neither Ralph nor I could resist misbehaving for the scowling nun, and eventually we exhausted Father Brian's patience. After one particularly trying incident, Father Brian resorted to parental involvement. He gave us notes to take to our parents, and he admonished us to not return to catechism or Mass until he'd heard from our parents. I was terrified. My mother was strict and my new stepfather was unforgiving. If they knew I'd been misbehaving in church, my summer would be ruined—they'd punish me for weeks! I left the rectory on the verge of tears. Ralph, though, was completely unaffected by the dilemma. He skipped across the parking lot, laughing and whistling. He was acting as if Father Brian had given us letters of commendation to take home. When he noticed that I was near tears, Ralph asked me what was wrong.

"They're gonna kill me," was all I could choke out.

"Don't worry, Pal, they're not even gonna know," and with that, Ralph *opened the sealed envelope* and began to read the letter out loud. "Oh, my old man's never gonna see this," he told me as he ripped up the letter and throwing it into the storm drain.

Before I could protest, Ralph plucked my letter from my hands and deposited it in the storm drain with his. Then he told me his plan: he and I would meet at the bottom of the hill from the church, then we'd kill time until Mass let out and walk home as if we'd been at the service. Every Sunday morning Ralph and I would meet at the corner of East Main Street and Second Street, but instead of walking *up the hill* to church, we'd walk *down the hill* to the Five and Dime. The best solution we could find for the collection plate money that our mothers gave us every week was to spend it!

So Ralph and began skipping church. We'd eat ice cream sundaes and penny candy, and we'd walk down to the bridge to throw rocks into the Youghiogheny River while we told each other that we weren't afraid of being caught. Around 11:45 AM we'd amble back up the hill to wait for the crowd—the people leaving the 10:45 AM Mass at Holy Family Catholic Church—the mass Ralph and I were *supposed* to be attending—the mass both of our parents *thought* we were attending.

Ralph and I would bid each other farewell, and I'd walk up the hill alone, and prepare myself for my mother's inevitable questions. How was Mass? *Fine, Ma.* What did the Father talk about today? *Not to sin, Ma.* As a last resort I would pretend that I didn't understand the sermon. I was, after all, only eight years old. But I managed to pull it off for the whole summer. Labor Day came and went, and Ralph and I went back to school. We only saw each other occasionally at recess and on Sunday mornings. I began to relax. Ice cream and penny candy became the norm. I no longer worried about getting caught.

I hadn't factored Alice's baptism into my plan. In late September, my parents took little Alice to the church to arrange it. At the end of their meeting, Father Brian asked, "So I guess you decided not to send Benny back to church until you returned?" I was busted.

I did get punished, but it wasn't nearly as bad as I thought it was going to be. In the end I was given a choice: I could go to church on Sundays, or I could stay home—it was entirely up to me. I chose to stay home and play—what eight-year-old wouldn't? And I was happy until somewhere around Thanksgiving. With every passing Sunday, I'd think about what I was missing. By mid-December I was back at Mass—voluntarily!

Forty years later, I'm still attending Mass every Sunday. What I didn't realize when I was eight years old (and stealing the collection money) was that I was stealing from God—stealing opportunities to help others less fortunate than myself. Believe me, now that I'm adding to the collection basket, ice cream sundaes and penny candy taste much better!

Words in a Pantry

By Nikki Loftin

My eight-year-old son, Cameron, followed me into the pantry to talk, so I knew it was serious.

"Mom, I don't want to go to church anymore."

"Why not? What's happened?"

"None of my friends go. They don't even believe in God."

"Honey, what's really going on? I thought you liked our new church."

A guilty look. "I only like the doughnuts."

I sat down on the boxes that lined the wall, boxes from my office, from the nine years I had spent working in churches as the Director of Children's Ministries. For years, I had felt called by God to teach His children. Eighteen months ago, I felt Him calling me to another task. When I first felt the tug away from our lovely church, our friends and family, I ignored it. God doesn't like to be ignored, and He made things increasingly uncomfortable for me until I threw my hands up and (to quote one of the songs that He used to pester me with during those months) "let Jesus take the wheel."

I doubted everything: whether we would be able to live without my salary, whether it was the right time, whether it was best for my family, whether we would be able to find a new church. I had given hundreds of children's sermons during those nine years, and now, in my doubt-filled pantry, I couldn't find the right words to help my own child.

"None of your friends believe?"

He shook his head. "They don't even think there is a God. And I don't want them to know I'm a Christian. They'll think I *pray* all the time. Sean will think I'm weird." Sean was his new best friend.

I didn't have the words, not the right words. But God did.

That Wednesday, my five-year-old son asked for Bible stories at bedtime. Daniel had just been thrown into the lion's den when Sean and Cameron wandered in to listen. Sean looked curious, and crawled up on the bed to listen.

"Do you know this story, Sean?"

"No," Cameron interrupted. "Sean doesn't believe in God."

"Really," I asked. "You don't?" Sean shook his head no.

My five-year-old swiveled around, a look of amazement on his face. "But God's real!" A shout, unqualified, brave, and true. The faith of a child, my child. Sean looked at Cameron with an unspoken question. Cameron nodded, just a little.

And then my doubts were gone. The children's sermons I had given all those years were to children who believed, mostly, who knew He was real. But here, in my own home, He sent me a child who needed to hear His story, who did not believe. This is what I had been practicing for all along. I dragged Daniel back out of the lion's den, and started the story over at the beginning. All three boys listened intently: Sean with wide eyes, Cameron with a tiny smile.

That night, I opened my Bible to Luke 15, and fell asleep reading about lost sheep, lost coins, and lost children, knowing that no matter how lost Cameron and I felt, there was no doubt that God was still there, finding us again and again.

The Church of the Holy Dunkin' Donuts

By Pierre O'Rourke

Mom used to say that I was the only child she knew who was sent from class in elementary school to see the school principal and from Sunday school to see the minister. Generally, it was for one of my "observations" or a question the Sunday school teacher felt would "take too much of the class time to explain."

One of the first times I was sent to see Reverend Dan was a couple of weeks before our Easter Pageant. At my young age, the whole cross thing hit me as rather gross. When I questioned why my Catholic friends went so far as to hang crosses with dead Jesus on them, I was sent to Reverend Dan. It seemed to me that the big thing about Jesus wasn't that He died on a cross but that He woke up and was able to push a big boulder out of the entrance to the cave to keep on teaching in the world. In my wee mind I figured it took no talent to kill someone but something special to wake from the dead. When Reverend Dan asked me what I would use as a symbol, I suggested we could use a rock or the circle shape of a rock.

Dan listened quite patiently. He pulled on his suit jacket, commented that there was still an hour until church began, and invited me to run an errand with him. That errand was the first of many we made together to Dunkin' Donuts. Using cinnamon sticks, Dan explained the cross to me in a way that made sense. But he admitted that there were more stones and rocks than there were crosses in the world, and that he did like the idea I had about the circle created by the shape of a rock. So he told me if I could better imagine God when I saw rocks or stones or circles, that it was just fine with him, and probably with God too.

There seemed to be frequent "go to the minister's office" events involving me. I would arrive from class carrying a note from the teacher; Reverend Dan would pull at his jaw, read the note, fold it twice to put in his side pocket, and then tell his secretary he had an errand to run. As time went by, Dunkin' Donuts became the pulpit from which Reverend Dan would share God's message. Once I got into a fight over having an accent and no father. Fighting in Sunday school was a big no-no, regardless of the reason. After cleaning my broken lip, Reverend Dan used various kinds of jelly doughnuts to illustrate how we may look different on the outside but are all the same on the inside. We used seven of them to make sure I got that lesson right.

A question of different religions and why we had missionaries had us headed back to Dunkin' Donuts, where this time we were allowed in the kitchen. There, Reverend Dan showed how the baker began with one huge ball of dough and how his hand shaped so many individual things. They all appeared different but were all still part of the original creation. Afterward, Reverend Dan convinced the clerk to let him put a business card in any bags sold, with a note to call and let us know how far the doughnuts had traveled. It was a great experiment, and he also netted a few more churchgoers with that one.

It was my question on a Father's Day about why some dads became drunks and were so mean to mothers that was the cause for another note that took me to Reverend Dan's office. This time when we arrived at Dunkin' Donuts he showed me the baker's oven. With the heat washing my face and fresh bakery smells surrounding us, he explained that how long the doughnuts were left in the oven as well as their placement on the shelf governed how soft or how hard they became. Slowly, I began to understand that my dad, and bullies in general, were a product of their environment. Reverend Dan gathered up our order and found us a place to sit. He went on to explain that our decisions and actions have the power to change what can seem to be inevitable. To illustrate his point he dipped a hard doughnut in his hot cup of coffee, rendering it as tasty as the soft ones, the same way love and kindness can transform a hardened heart.

On another trip, I began to get a grasp of why God was called Our Father and that His holy parentship was not a regional thing. Another excursion had him use the doughnut holes to show how their centers got separated but could still be brought together; this was illustrated by us eating them.

My Uncle Kermit died when he was quiet young, and I got mad at the teacher when she said, "It's okay; he's with God now." Frankly, I was mad at God as I carried that pass to the minister. As our doughnuts arrived, Reverend Dan shared a lesson I would be reminded of years later when I watched the film, *Phenomenon*. He gently took my half-eaten doughnut from my hand, leaving me to stare with my mouth open. He looked at the dripping jelly as if it were the Holy Grail and said, "So, if I set this doughnut down it will get all hard and stuck to the plate and not even the birds will want it. But if we both take bites of it," as he ate half of what remained, "then . . . it becomes part of us forever. And no one can take that away from you or me." He handed the doughnut back and I slowly finished it.

"And what your Uncle Kermit gave you, and gave me, and gave his friends at the church, well, that will be a part of us forever."

Reverend Dan died recently and I never had the chance to thank him for those quality days we spent at the Church of the Holy Dunkin' Donuts. He knew how impressions made upon a little boy and young man are the ones that often get carried through an entire life. He was also aware of how often God gets blocked out, so he made sure my difficult questions did not get me sidelined in life. Thanks to Reverend Dan, I knew that God was still around and a part of my foundation. And Reverend Dan is too—still around in my heart and a part of my foundation.

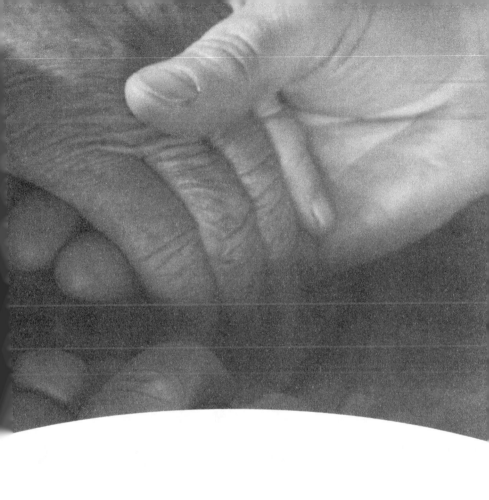

Making
a Difference

His Parish on Wheels

By Kay Presto

The priest raised the host in full reverence. I bowed my head in prayer. It was Sunday Mass, and I was grateful to be here to share this respect to God. As I received Communion, the background sounds began. They continued to grow louder and louder. These were not the sounds of a choir or an organ. These were the high-pitched sounds of Indy Car engines, as the open-wheel cars began their practice session on the road course at California's Mazda Raceway Laguna Seca.

It was 1985, and I was blessed to be able to attend Mass and receive my Communion right at the racetrack. The priest? Father Phil DeRea. He travels the Indy Car Series circuit, bringing God to reporters like myself who cannot get to a church located miles away while covering the races.

"Father Phil," as he's fondly known, is quickly recognizable as he says his Mass. He's the only priest known to administer the sacraments while wearing a black-and-white checkered stole, in semblance of a checkered racing flag. His original stole was created for him in his hometown of Nazareth, Pennsylvania, by a woman named Irene Jany, but that one wore out from many years of use. His current stole was made by Sparco, the same company that makes racers' fire-retardant suits. Because he's constantly at one racetrack or another all racing season long, it fits his holy image perfectly.

Since 1971, he's been bringing Mass and the sacraments to racetracks throughout the United States and in foreign countries. I've attended his services in tiny trailers, hospitality areas, in a room near the media center, and in open-air pavilions. Wherever Father DeRea is, I follow, to receive my God while I'm working at the tracks.

One year, at the Toyota Grand Prix in Long Beach, California, I was extremely concerned. I was doing a radio broadcast every half-hour from the street course. How would I ever find him at that huge sprawling facility? As luck would have it, he was scheduled to say Mass right across the hall from where I was broadcasting! Imagine my joy as I dashed across the hall, attended Mass, received Communion, and still completed my next broadcast on-air. That started my day off with a wonderful and blessed feeling, as I had once again been able to begin it with God.

Father Phil's life is a hectic one—shuttling from one race track to another throughout the entire Indy Car Series racing season, and also trying to fit in funerals, weddings, baptisms, and other ministries as a missionary of the Sacred Heart at his home base in Aurora, Illinois. "Often, a couple getting married in Aurora will plan their wedding date to accommodate *my* racing schedule," he says, with a chuckle.

It's not just reporters who need his services. "One group who really benefits from having Mass at the track are the drivers of the race transporters," he pointed out to me one day. "They can't drive their huge transporters to a nearby church, so it's a special benefit to them." At his services, one will see all types of people—race drivers, their families, team publicists, crew members, mechanics, even young boys and girls, and people who are not Catholic. "The people feel very close to me," he says, "especially the children, and they all come to pray. People always tell me what a comfort it is to be able to attend these Masses. They definitely become my parishioners." As a member of the Pontifical Council for People on the Move, which also covers circus and carnival workers, he performs baptisms and even weddings at various racetracks.

He's also there in time of urgent need. One weekend, two drivers were involved in a racing accident. Both were hospitalized due to their injuries. Father DeRea was immediately there to administer to them. "It was a wonderful connection for them," he says. "They felt a certain peace, and began talking about God and how He watched over them. Instead of their saying, 'I can't drive, I'm injured,' they said, 'God was good to me. I'll be able to drive again. I'll be able to continue my work.' So there's a special presence there. We have the physical, psychological, and now the spiritual dimension to their racing."

And when he's not at the racetrack? Father Phil is still in high gear. In Aurora, this dedicated cleric also serves as director of development for fundraisers that raise money for Sacred Heart missionaries overseas. One of his current projects is helping to build a seminary school for twenty-four students in Colombia, South America. Other projects that benefit from his efforts are aiding elderly priests and brothers, and helping schools and hospitals in Papua, New Guinea. He seems to be almost everywhere, bringing the word of God to others whenever necessary.

After 41 years, he still has tremendous enthusiasm for his work. "What's so great is how people accept me and want me to be part of their lives there at the racetrack," he says with his usual warm grin. "I find it most inspiring to administer the sacraments to the people who are there. That is not something a person ordinarily finds in another sport. To bring God to the track is so important."

His church may not be a cathedral, but his reverence makes every service feel like it's being held in one. And no matter where he's saying Mass, this wonderful and caring priest helps me keep my faith—and the faith of thousands of others—grounded and very much alive. Through his outstanding dedication to God, he has taught me to pass on his enduring example to others, and to enjoy God's blessings—even at the tracks.

No Just
Another Drive-By

By Kristen Feola

The red light kept our car at the intersection where the two girls stood. I glanced over at the cardboard sign that one held. The sign's message, in thick black marker, was the typical one—something about being homeless? *Sure*, I thought. *Whatever.*

I quickly looked away. My five-year-old daughter didn't.

"Mommy, what are those girls doing there? And what does their sign say?" she asked. Keeping my eyes on the road, I attempted to explain that those girls didn't have a place to live and needed help. Isabelle was quiet as she thought about my answer. Since she is by nature very inquisitive, I fully expected her to keep asking questions like she normally does. Instead, there was silence—silence that forced me to make a decision. Finally, the light turned green. I drove away, but my thoughts were still on those girls.

On any other day, I probably wouldn't have given them a second thought. Usually when I see someone standing beside the road asking for money, I tend to be pretty skeptical. I'm not proud of that fact, but I'm just being honest. I wonder if such people are truly impoverished, or if they're just out to scam anyone who feels sorry for them. I also question how they would spend the money if I did give it to them. Would they put it toward groceries or bills, or go on a shopping spree for beer, drugs, and lottery tickets?

That day, though, instead of being judgmental, I was moved with compassion. Those girls on the corner couldn't have been more than eighteen years old. They looked so young and vulnerable. Questions raced through my mind. What was their story? Why were they homeless? And, then the one gnawing question that thrust me out of my comfort zone and into their world: What if those were my nieces, or cousins . . . or *daughters* standing on that corner?

I sensed the Lord's prompting and returned to the intersection. As I drove toward them I prayed, "God, I don't know what I can do. Give me wisdom. Show me how You want to bless them."

I parked the car in the lot next to where they stood and walked up to them. Their eyes were filled with sadness and fatigue, yet held a glimmer of hope as they saw me get out of my car. I started with, "Good morning," and then asked them what was going on in their lives.

Their names were Shannon and Melony, and they were roommates. Both were unemployed and about to be being evicted from their apartment since they couldn't pay their rent. I learned that Shannon was a single mother of a six-year-old son, and she was also on disability. Both were new to the area and didn't know anyone. Neither girl had a car, so they were riding the bus around town, trying to hit as many busy intersections as possible to make some money.

I admired their boldness. It took a great deal of courage to stand on the side of the road with a sign that basically shouts, "I can't do it on my own! I failed! I need help!" None of us likes to admit dependence upon anyone or anything. We want to do it ourselves, to make our own way. Desperation, though, often causes us to do things we wouldn't normally do. We swallow our pride, step out into the unknown, and take a chance by doing something risky.

As I listened to their plight, I brainstormed ideas on how I could help. I immediately thought of One Heart, a ministry at our church, which gives bags of groceries and personal care items to people in need. And I was going to the church that morning.

I told Shannon and Melony I'd pick up two bags of groceries for them. They seemed thankful and genuinely appreciative. I had a feeling that my offer of assistance was the first one they'd received all day.

We exchanged cell phone numbers, and I told them I'd drop off the groceries later in the day. As I drove on to the church, I was energized. I knew I had done what the Lord wanted me to do. However, I started thinking about why I'd never stopped to help anyone like them in the past and why this time was different.

Earlier that morning I had sat at my kitchen table reading Ephesians 2:1-10. As I sat there thinking about God's grace, I was overwhelmed with how much He loves me. I wrote the following reflection in my journal:

> *The Word says that it is by this amazing grace that we are saved. So,*
> *what is this grace? Grace is not a prayer of thanksgiving offered up*
> *before we eat. Grace is God's kindness poured out to us in the person*

of Jesus Christ. Like Ephesians 2 says, without Jesus we are dead in our sins. We are caught up in the ways of this world, seeking pleasure in things that do not satisfy. Our lives are spiraling out of control, without direction and without hope. But, God doesn't just leave us in our pitiful condition. He calls out to us, offering this free gift of salvation to anyone who will receive it. He points to the cross and to the work His Son did on our behalf. All we have to do is believe that Jesus died for our sins. He is the One who paid the price and made a way for us to have a relationship with God.

And, just so that we don't begin to think more of ourselves than we ought, God reminds us that this saving grace is "not by works, so that no one can boast (Ephesians 2)." Aaah, He knows us so well. God doesn't even give us a chance to become prideful when it comes to our salvation. He makes it clear that it is by grace we are saved. Grace alone!

The Lord had led me to those verses to prepare my heart for what would come later in the day. God showed me through His Word that His grace *always* demands a response.

His gift of salvation is not to be taken lightly. The Lord has saved me, not only to rescue me from eternal separation from Him but also so that I will share His unconditional love and truth with those around me. So when I saw those two young girls standing there, I couldn't just drive on by. How could I when the Lord has done so much for me? If I am too busy, too distracted, and too selfish to reach out to help someone else in need, then I know nothing of Christ's love. As the Word says in John 13:34, "Love one another. As I have loved you, so you must love one another."

The Lord opened the eyes of my heart today. He enlarged my vision so that I didn't just see homeless girls standing beside the road, holding a cardboard sign. Instead, I saw them through Jesus' eyes—two hurting souls in need of compassion and hope.

Out of the Zone

By Rachel Allord

It started with a simple question.

"Rachel, can I ask you a favor?" my friend Frank said as I stepped into our church's sanctuary on a Sunday morning.

"Of course," I replied, thinking he was going to ask me to check on his kids in the nursery or relay a message to his wife.

"Can you sit with Corinne today?"

Although I had never officially met her before, I knew who Corinne was. She was confined to a wheelchair, and her nursing home dropped her off at the front door of our church each Sunday morning. A gracious couple from our church took care of her from there.

Frank's request sent my heart racing. As much as I hate to admit it, I turn into a nervous wreck around people who are ill or have special needs, and unless it's to visit a newborn baby, I aim to stay away from hospitals. Even caroling through a nursing home has set my pulse racing.

"Her caregivers aren't here today and she needs someone to sit with her," Frank continued. "Maybe you could sit next to her during service and make sure she's okay? It can be difficult to understand what she's saying sometimes but if you lift up her arms periodically it alleviates the pressure on her lungs or something and she can speak easier. I would do it but I'm playing keyboard today."

I decided to shoot straight. "I don't know. This is way out of my comfort zone."

"Okay. I understand."

"I mean, I'd seriously rather preach the sermon." But before I even finished the statement I felt the ugliness of my words. *What's wrong with me? Can't I step out of my comfort zone to help someone? I'm even the wife of one of the pastors, for crying out loud!* "Okay, I'll do it," I relented, more to the Lord than to Frank.

Ignoring the butterflies that were body-slamming inside my stomach, I settled myself in the chair next to Corinne's wheelchair and managed a wobbly smile. "Hi, I'm Rachel. Can I sit with you today?"

Corinne looked at me in alarm. I was a stranger to her.

"Your caregivers weren't able to be here today but I can help you," I said hoping to convince myself.

I sang along with the worship music and Corinne made her own sounds. At first I thought she was, in her own way, singing too. But her guttural sounds became louder, more frantic, and when I glanced at her I saw that her face was red and perspiring. Leaning over to her I asked what was wrong, but I couldn't understand her garbled speech. As the worship leader ended the song and launched into a corporate prayer, Corinne's moaning intensified. Panic washed over me. Maybe I should wheel her out to the foyer. Standing, I tried to move her chair but it was locked and I had no idea how to unlock it. Corinne wailed again. Still leading the prayer, the worship leader's eyes locked on mine and I felt my face flush. It was as if all eight-hundred eyes were focused on me and the scene I couldn't get under control. I wanted to shout to Frank, who was helplessly sitting behind the keyboard, that I had changed my mind; I couldn't do this after all. He gazed at me empathetically over the head of the congregants as Corinne's wailing hit a crescendo.

Then suddenly I remembered; Frank had said something about Corinne's arms. I lifted the arm closest to me, cradling her heavy forearm in my palm, my elbow resting on top of the arm of her wheelchair. Her moaning ceased and after a few minutes I tiptoed around her wheelchair to relieve the other one. Corinne let out a sigh, clearly relieved that I finally recognized her need. We worked out a routine for the rest of the service; when she made a certain grunt I knew it was time to lift an arm. We did this throughout the service and my heart grieved over the frustration Corinne must feel to have to rely on someone to simply lift her arms.

I was too focused on the task at hand to pay attention to the sermon that day. At the end of service I gave Corinne's shoulder a gentle squeeze and told her it was nice to sit with her. Her blue eyes met mine and she said almost inaudibly but sincerely, "Thank you."

As I turned away, back to my normal life, down the Sunday school hall to retrieve my kids and then on to find my husband, I was humbled and somber, simultaneously proud and disappointed with my attitude, my actions, myself. Stepping into someone else's shoes—especially ones that are as cumbersome as Corrine's—can be disconcerting, even if it is only for an hour and fifteen minutes.

If I'm being truthful, helping Corinne was painfully uncomfortable and notably awkward. In fact, Corinne would probably prefer that I never do it again. Her usual caregivers—and probably a good handful of our congregants—are better equipped to meet Corinne's needs and serve her with dignity. I did my best but it was not my finest hour. Like everyone, I suppose, I'd much rather stick to what I know: to the ministries in which I'm confident or gifted, and serve in areas in which I can see some amount of success.

But ultimately, serving is not about me. It's about *serving*. And sometimes, ministry opportunities refuse to neatly fit into a "giftedness" category; they simply require a compassionate heart and a healthy dose of humility—two fruits of the Spirit I'm thankful Corinne cultivated in me.

You Are So Loved

By Nicole Bromley

"You are so loved." These four words would one day penetrate my heart and mind, and leave a mark on my future. But these are the same four words that, for many years, went in one ear and out the other, for they didn't match my circumstances. But Pastor Joe didn't know that. To him, my circumstances didn't change this obvious truth. To him, I was so loved . . . no matter what.

Pastor Joe had a gentleness about him unlike that of any man I had ever met. His voice was soft, his words were kind, his smile was inviting, and his heart was caring. I first came to know him on the weekends I had scheduled visits with my father, when I was a young girl. I enjoyed Pastor Joe and his church, but I was unable to fully embrace them because so much of my energy was spent focusing on the mask I felt I had to wear in public. I forced myself to create an image of a perfect, innocent little girl—a mask I wore to keep my inner pain and confusion from being outwardly seen.

It wasn't until I was a teenager that I found the courage to remove that mask. For nearly a decade I had been sexually abused by my stepfather, and the silent pain and torment were released with great fear of what others would think of me. Although Pastor Joe wasn't the first person I revealed my secret to, he played a major role in my escape to freedom. Pastor Joe was a silent hero, always waiting in the wings, always there when you needed him. He quietly gave money to those in need when he himself had none. Years later, I learned that on occasion he had driven to my house when no one was there to pray over our home and our family. And always, always, he spoke words of kindness and truth over me, even when I couldn't accept them.

For nearly twenty years, every time I saw Pastor Joe he would greet me with the warmest, proud-father kind of smile, always followed by the words, "Nicole, you are so loved." I heard these words from his voice. I also saw them in his eyes, and I felt them in his safe, fatherly embrace. But like a kicked puppy, I was still fearful. In the back of my mind, I wondered if Pastor Joe would end up being another scary man who could not be trusted and who was only out for his own pleasure. But as the years went by, I learned Pastor Joe was a man to be trusted. His heart was pure. His hands were loving, his eyes were caring, and his voice spoke the truth.

Earlier this year, Pastor Joe fought a long battle with cancer and died only a few months ago. His hair turned a silvery gray and his body became thin and weak. Even though he was in a great deal of pain and the fight pulled him away from much of his public ministry, his kind words and warm smile never changed. He died only a few months ago. Because of Joe, I have seen Jesus in a very special way. The gentleness and compassion of Jesus was

exemplified in Pastor Joe, and brought me deep emotional healing, enabling me to trust men again and to be able to enter into
the happy, healthy marriage I have now. More than that, Pastor
Joe helped me to accept that I am truly loved. *No matter what.*
He helped me present my broken heart to God for healing and
restoration. Now I can truly love others, just as Pastor Joe did.

Pastor Joe was always there to do all he could to support me. He
was one of my biggest fans, a proud father figure always ready to
brag about my endeavors to anyone who would listen. But more
than all of that, he cared about me. He cared about my heart and
my mind and my personal walk with the Lord. He would buy
lunch at our favorite Mexican restaurant and we would talk about
what God was doing in me, not just through me. His utmost concern was for my heart. He longed for me to know more than anything that I was loved, and he encouraged me to live and serve
others from that identity.

I have no doubt that one man, one pastor of one small community can impact thousands around the world. Joe's kindness to
one young girl, mixed with his own moral integrity, has not only
changed one life, but has made a difference in the lives of many.
A few years ago I began a ministry of my own in which I travel
around the world, speaking to people, young and old, spreading a
message of hope and healing. Through the words I speak, the
books I write, through my eyes, my hugs, my everything, I seek to
help other victims of sexual abuse realize they, too, are loved. My
ministry has reached hundreds of thousands of silently hurting
people and has left a profound impact on churches and commu-
nities around the world.

Though he is no longer physically present, the impact of Pastor Joe's life here will never die. His ministry continues to influence my own. Today, as I miss this dear friend and one of the truest father figures I have found here on earth, I think of his life and his service to the church and our community as a whole. I believe that in his final breaths here on earth, he heard those same words resonating deep within his own heart and soul: "Pastor Joe, you are so loved."

A Voice from the Past

By Jewell Johnson

When my husband retired after forty-two years as a pastor, a long adjustment period followed. As LeRoy reflected on his years in ministry, he began to second guess all the time he had spent working for God. *Did I do any good?* LeRoy asked himself. *Is there any lasting fruit from those years? Did I help even one person?*

A few years later we received a special phone call. "Does a Pastor Johnson live at this number?" a hesitant voice asked. As LeRoy talked on the phone, I realized this was Cindy Parker—a voice from the past.

We had first become acquainted with Cindy when she was a five years old. LeRoy and I, recently married, were planting a church in the hills of southern Missouri. In an effort to contact non-churched families, we combed the countryside, calling on every farm family in the area. One day we stopped our car on the top of a grassy knoll where several children were playing in the yard. With a baby on her hip, and a toddler clinging to her skirt, Mrs. Parker answered our knock.

"We're starting a new church in town," LeRoy explained.

"We'd be happy to pick up your children for Sunday school." Mrs. Parker quickly agreed.

Every Sunday for five years, LeRoy drove the six miles to the farm on the grassy knoll, packed the five Parker kids into the backseat, and brought them to the storefront church. Cindy sat with other children around tables in a back room and listened to stories about Jesus. Each summer we held an all-day Vacation Bible School for a week. Linda, with her brothers and sisters, faithfully attended. They memorized Bible verses and sang scripture choruses. They heard Bible stories. And when an invitation was given to accept Christ, Cindy invited Jesus to live in her heart. And now here she was, talking on the phone with LeRoy after all these years.

As the two talked on the phone that day, LeRoy discovered Cindy had married, moved to California, and raised a family. "I want to thank you for taking us to church," she told him. "I've never stopped going." Now she worked as a volunteer in a church office where she had access to pastors' phone numbers, and that's how she'd found us.

Did Cindy understand what the call meant to her former pastor? Probably not, but no doubt she recognized the voice she had first heard as a child, and called to thank the person who had helped her begin a walk with God—a marvelous walk that had spanned over fifty years. She couldn't have chosen a better time to call.

Never Judge a Book by Its Cover

By Ava Pennington

M r. Kasses scared me half to death.

My life followed a set routine with few surprises. Monday to Friday, my sister and I went to school, Dad went to work, and Mom was the glue that held us together. Before I entered the fourth grade at the ripe old age of nine, all of my teachers had been women. For the preceding five years, from September through June, someone who looked like she could be my mother or grandmother taught me reading, writing, and arithmetic.

We weren't churchgoers. Sunday mornings were for sleeping late. The family Bible sat on a shelf—I don't remember it ever being opened. Then one day my aunt decided that my sister and I were missing an important part of life and that we should attend church. Actually, she brought us to Sunday school. And the teacher for fourth through sixth grade Sunday school was . . . a *man*! Not just any man, but one who looked as if he were old enough to be my grandfather's father. Mr. Kasses moved slowly and had thinning gray hair. Time had left its mark, etching a host of wrinkles on his face. A generous sprinkling of age spots joined those wrinkles on his face as well as on his hands.

Sunday school classes were held in the fellowship hall of the church, each class in its own corner, partitioned by curtains. The small building was simple and sturdy. An old furnace provided heat in the winter. During the summer, the only cooling came from huge industrial fans on tall poles that pushed hot, humid air around the room. Even so, every Sunday Mr. Kasses arrived dressed the same way, in a crisply pressed suit complete with white shirt, tie, and jacket.

He had a well-deserved reputation for being a stickler for the rules. And he had a *lot* of rules. We had to arrive on time, no grace period for lateness. We had to bring our Bibles to class every week. We had to complete our homework—*Sunday school homework!*—every week.

Of course, this wasn't the first time I'd been in a classroom with a teacher who had rules. But until now my teachers had been extremely understanding—you might even say nurturing—when we students didn't meet their standards. After all, we were only children. But Mr. Kasses did not believe in coddling. He treated us like young adults, not little children. He communicated high standards of behavior and expected us to comply, without explanation, excuse, or exception.

I didn't like this at all, especially the part about homework. In fact I wondered if he even had a right to do it. Surely there had to be a law somewhere that said only *real* teachers (the Monday-to-Friday kind) were allowed to assign homework!

But Mr. Kasses also intrigued me. He wasn't quite what he appeared to be. Maybe it was the way he took the time to answer our questions, never belittling us or making us feel like we had asked a stupid question. Maybe it was the way his eyes lit up when we finally grasped a particular detail, his head nodding slowly as if he had never heard the truth we had just discovered for ourselves. Maybe it was my amazement when I overheard someone say that it was Mr. Kasses—Mr. *Kasses!*—who purchased the candy that was distributed to all the children in our church every Christmas.

Most of all, it was the way he held his Bible. He carried a big, heavy, leather Bible. The rest of us, children and adults, carried our Bibles as we would any other book. Not Mr. Kasses. He held his Bible reverently, he turned the pages gently, and he read each word with an obviously cherished respect for the Author. His Bible was more than *a* book to him—it was *the* book. He quoted verses and principles from it in answer to every one of our questions. I also sensed, without him actually saying it, that this same Book was the source of answers for his own questions. No matter what the subject, he knew where to look. It was his precious possession—his anchor—and I was determined to find out why.

I wanted what Mr. Kasses had—real, time-tested, unshakable faith. Knowledge and understanding of his Bible had provided a solid foundation and a calm assurance for his faith during his long and sometimes difficult life. My life was just beginning, but I knew he had something I needed. He birthed a spark in me and then fanned the flame to hunger for something more.

Mr. Kasses was the first teacher to treat me like a young lady instead of a child. And he expected me to behave accordingly. But his impact on my life is much more significant than that. He taught me to look beyond myself to seek my life's purpose. And he pointed me to a relationship with the Creator of the Universe—the one who loved me enough to send His Son, Jesus Christ, to die for me.

Not everyone believed as he did, but that didn't bother him. Our doubts and questions didn't trouble him, either—not even when one of the boys in our class told him he thought these were nice stories, but *only* stories. Never once did I hear Mr. Kasses argue or raise his voice or belittle someone else's beliefs. Still, his own never wavered.

For three years he taught me, and the others in my class, that the Bible is not just another book. He prepared me for the turbulent teenage years by giving me my very own anchor. That anchor protected me from making the wrong choices many of my friends made. It helped me to see a world beyond my own difficult circumstances. For that I am eternally grateful.

I now have the privilege of teaching and writing about my own faith and how others can also have a relationship with the Creator of the Universe. Mr. Kasses' legacy lives on. Someday, I will have the opportunity to thank him.

Running for Two

By Carol M. Benthal-Bingley

If you've shared a good run with someone, you've created a bond with that person for life. We runners have a bond because we share something in common. We have a connection beyond the surface. We've seen each other at our best and our worst. We've seen each other physically and emotionally drained from pushing ourselves farther than we thought we could be pushed. We push each other, and when we fall, we pick each other up. We're part of a unique community, a family of runners with all our strengths and beautiful flaws.

I met Annie, a dear friend of my sister, about five years ago. She was a beautiful woman . . . talented, energetic, bright, vibrant, and she was a runner. I wasn't much of a runner at the time, but I wanted to be. She helped me train for and race my first triathalon. She was amazing: strong, elegant—and dying of cancer.

Last year, around the time her doctor had given her only two more months to live, I bumped into Annie. She asked me to run for her until she could run again. She shared how she'd missed running; how she missed feeling the breeze in her hair as she ran;

how she longed to go out and just run, and keep on running.

A group of us decided to run for Annie. We logged miles and miles for our "sister." We offered up the run for our friend. We had a bond with her, through her, to do something outside of ourselves. To offer up that run to whomever it is we pray to. We were running for two. Running for someone else, someone who missed running desperately. We started out doing it for her and quickly realized how much she was doing for us. She was giving us strength, inspiring us every step of the way.

Annie died a few weeks ago. This incredible woman had been given two years to live—that was six years ago. She was given six months a few years ago. Her endurance was beyond anything we could imagine. When she was given forty-eight hours, she took another week. She fought all the way to the finish line. Her body was done, but something way beyond physical strength took over. She stayed on this earth longer, running toward her own finish line, not giving in until her race was won.

My friend Julie and I decided to run another race in honor of Annie. It was a beautiful day, a Sunday, a day Annie would have loved to run. We ran to the first-mile marker, slapped hands, and decided to whom we'd dedicate each mile as it came. We ran for Annie, her lovely daughter, her two brave sons, her loving husband, her dear "sisters", and for Annie again. We rotated through the people whom Annie loved. It was such an emotional, spiritual journey running through those woods, gaining steam at each mile. We thought about the endurance this woman had, the strength she showed as she faced her own mortality, and the dignity and grace she wore as she fought this unimaginable battle. When we had thoughts of doubt and pain and feeling tired, we thought of Annie. We know that the small amount of endurance we exhibited that day was nothing compared to the race Annie had just completed.

By mile eight, I was tired. When the next mile marker came up, Julie and I regrouped, slapped hands, and said, "This one's for Annie." I started off on the second half of the run, winding through the trees, the sun spilling through the leaves. I closed my eyes for a second, consciously breathing in the fresh air. Just then something filled me up—I felt lighter, energized, refilled. I cannot give credit to my sports drink or energy gels for this one. This was beyond the chemistry of complex carbs and electrolytes. I believe I felt the presence of something bigger and the warmth of knowing that Annie was smiling and probably somewhere out there . . . running! I finished the race, worn out and filled up. I watched for Julie. She came cruising in with an amazing energy and a decisive surge at the finish. We were exhausted and energized, laughing and crying. She shared how she'd pooped out the last mile and a half, thinking she wouldn't finish.

She said she'd just flown in on Annie's wings.

Home for Christmas

By Lynne Gentry

When my husband received the call to pastor a downtown church in a small southern Georgia community, he was excited. I was not. To me, moving so far from our Midwestern roots would require sacrifice. The meager salary would never stretch to cover the cost of holiday travel. Living in the South meant my kids would not see their grandparents or snow on Christmas morning. Visions of our young children learning to replace "you" with "y'all" popped into my head. Raising my family this far from home was not what I'd signed up for.

But what choice did I have? We'd been without a job for months and needed a paycheck. So after we polished off my mom's Thanksgiving turkey, friends and family helped us pack the U-Haul with our two small kids and a dog. As we pulled away from everything we knew and loved, my children waved goodbye. I clung to the sack of Thanksgiving leftovers.

Two long days later, and almost a thousand miles from home, we parked the moving truck in the parsonage drive. I eyed our new home through the bug-splattered windshield. Large live oaks draped with Spanish moss shaded the two-story brick house—situated less than ten feet from a busy highway.

"Home, sweet home." My husband reached across the two sleeping children crammed between us and patted my leg. "I'll get the key." He jumped from the cab and bounded toward the church building next door.

Men can pack their underwear and feel moved, but I felt like a tree yanked from the dirt, my roots dying in the harsh elements. I climbed wearily from the cab and sunk ankle-deep into sandy soil. Humidity kinked my hair and the smell of wet paper from the nearby paper mills churned my stomach. Surveying our new neighborhood, I spotted a newspaper office to my left and the church parking to my right. In front of me, log trucks hauling Georgia pines rumbled past at fifty-five miles an hour, rattling the parsonage windows and my raw nerves.

Where would my children play? And with whom . . . the three-inch cockroaches scurrying along the sidewalk? Swallowing the disappointment rising in my throat, I noticed a ragged woman with matted hair hawking papers in front of the newspaper office. Her toothless grin didn't seem to offend the drivers who stopped at the intersection, but something about her unkempt appearance sent a ripple of unease down my spine. What had we gotten ourselves into?

Before I could jump back into the truck and make a run for it, excited church members descended on the U-Haul. Within a couple of hours they had us unloaded, dishes unpacked, and beds set up. I was officially stuck. I spent the next few weeks meeting a few people and eating lots of fried fish and cheese grits. Everyone seemed to go out of their way to make us feel welcome, but I still felt lonely and displaced. When I called Mom to whine, she suggested it might cheer me up to look past myself and find someone less fortunate. Instead, I set out to recreate my treasured holiday traditions, like chopping a live tree and making sugar cookies.

A few of days before Christmas, I pulled the last pan of golden cookies from the oven, the nostalgic smell of my mother's kitchen bringing tears to my eyes. "Once these cool, we'll ice them," I told my children as the doorbell rang.

Irritated because we couldn't have two minutes to ourselves, I stomped to the door and peered through the glass. The woman with the matted hair stood on the porch. A small, barefoot boy peeked around her leg. I recognized her as the lady my kids and I bought a newspaper from every evening. Maybe she thought we weren't coming today. Why hadn't I ever asked her name?

Shame flushed my cheeks as I opened the door. "Can I help you?"

"This the church house?"

"Yes."

She pushed the boy toward me. "My boy's hungry."

"Well, I—"

"I've been workin' two jobs to get my boy back. CPS says if I can't feed him, I can't keep him. He's all I got, lady." The desperation lighting her eyes pierced the dark place in my heart.

"Wait here." I rushed to the kitchen and tossed warm cookies into a bag. Next, I gathered several cans from the pantry and snatched the loaf of bread and a jar of peanut butter sitting on the counter. I raced back to the front door. "Do you live around here?"

"We got a room at that house behind the paper."

"The one without glass in the windows?"

She ducked her head, and I wished I hadn't blurted that out.

I handed her the groceries. "Merry Christmas."

"Same to y'all, lady." She balanced the bag on one hip and took her son's hand. "Come on, Timmy."

I watched them walk down the porch steps. Once they reached the bottom, the woman fished a cookie from the bag. Timmy gobbled it down, but she ate nothing as they headed toward the stack of papers on the corner.

I turned around to find my children watching and waiting to see what I would do.

"Will Santa bring that boy shoes, Momma?" my daughter asked.

Twinkling lights reflected off the shiny ribbons and bows on the presents stuffed under our Christmas tree. How could I have been so ungrateful? Even far from family, I had so much.

"Let's see what we can do."

For the next two days I plowed through the church directory, calling people I hadn't even met yet. I told them about Timmy and his mother. Gifts, money, and food poured into our living room. My children and I went shopping. Together we picked out a toy for Timmy, some clothes, and a pair of shoes.

On Christmas Eve, people crowded into our living room to help wrap the generous bounty. Our new home was filled with laughter and the smell of hot chocolate. I noticed I brimmed with something I hadn't expected—joy. We loaded our cars and drove around the corner to the house where ratty curtains billowed in the unusually chilly breeze. I climbed the steps and knocked on the door.

"Is Timmy home?" I asked the woman with the matted hair.

Cautiously she and Timmy followed me to the cars. Everyone's eyes were fastened on the two standing before our overloaded trunks.

Tears welled in the woman's eyes. "Y'all did this for us?"

My children thrust the present they'd wrapped into Timmy's hands. He clutched the package and fingered the shiny paper.

"Open it!" they shouted.

Timmy's mother put her arm around his thin shoulders. "He ain't never had a present before."

My children happily demonstrated how to rip paper from boxes. Soon shredded wrappings littered the ground. I helped Timmy wiggle into his new socks and shoes while others carried the gifts up to their little room.

Later that night, I rinsed the cocoa mugs and dropped into bed, exhausted yet giddy. Helping others with people committed to the same purpose felt like family.

Tomorrow was December 25. But tonight was Christmas. And I was home.

THE PINK ANGELS

3DAY
BENEFITING
THE SUSAN G. KOMEN
BREAST CANCER
FOUNDATION

A NATIONAL PHILANTHROPIC TRUST

w.The3Day.org

AST CANCER

Living the
Golden Rule

Dignity

By Nan Trammell Jones

I twisted my face into a phony smile—a little contorted, a lot deceptive. I was completely out of deodorant and had no choice but to borrow my husband's. The bright red container read FRESH SPORT.

Oh, great, I thought sarcastically. *I always wanted to smell like a jock.* Truth was, using my husband's deodorant was the last straw. We were in a financial crisis due to job loss. We had just purchased gas with five dollars and fifty cents in rolled *pennies* (the nickels, dimes, and quarters were long gone), our phone had been disconnected, we were almost out of food, and now—NOW(!)—I had to use men's deodorant!

"Lord," I complained aloud, "I am *not* happy. This is not the abundant life I was expecting." My sarcasm was out of control and then evolved into desperation. "Please, Lord, You promised to 'make a way where there seems to be no way.' This would be a good time to make things happen—I am at my wit's end!"

My tantrum evaporated into an exhausted hush.

In the marked silence I heard a familiar, quiet voice entreating me to trust and not be afraid. The presence of the Lord calmed me, His reassuring whisper comforted me. He reminded me that "all things work together for my good" and, in my spirit, I heard him speak of the eternal purposes He was weaving into my nightmare. I rested for a few moments in His peace.

"Honey, are you ready?" my husband called.

"Be right there."

We drove the two miles to our local food bank—the one we had supported for years—the same one that had invited my husband to serve on their board of directors. Can you imagine? Talk about a lesson in humility!

We both took a deep breath and pushed the door open. The entrance to the food bank was a physical door, but it was also a spiritual door, the beginning of a huge lesson, a God moment.

The director greeted us with a hug. She seemed a little taken aback that we had come in as clients, but her graciousness blanketed the awkwardness. My eyes brimmed with tears as we filled out the paper work. I could not believe the intensity of the battle that raged between my emotions and my faith. *Help me Lord. Help me to be thankful.*

Does that sound too simple? I have learned that thankfulness really is a key to coming through a crisis of this magnitude. A desire to be thankful kept me connected to my God. My thankful heart testified to my tormented mind that there was, and is, and always will be, a God who loves me—a God in whom I can place my hope.

We left that day with bologna and cheese, hot dogs, beans, and a new appreciation for people who have been stripped of their dignity and pride. Challenges know no boundaries. Despair can target anyone, anytime. And God's love? His love upholds, preserves, and restores. We felt encouraged as we drove away, not only with much-needed groceries, but also with a twenty-five dollar voucher for gas!

Later, as I unloaded the groceries, I saw something blue in the bottom of a bag—one lone stick of women's deodorant. Was God listening, or what?

We continued to pray and believe that things were going to turn around. And we were determined to find God's light in the midst of this darkness. The following week my husband was offered a full-time job with benefits. We began to move forward toward restoration, and we continue to look back on our lesson in thankfulness.

And what about eternal purposes?

I realized that as much as our bodies need food to survive, our spirits need dignity. Using men's deodorant was devastating for this girlie-girl. I am now making plans to start a basket ministry that will provide a touch of dignity for the struggling women who find themselves asking for mercy at the local food bank. The baskets will be filled with items such as women's deodorant, shampoo and conditioner, hairspray, nail polish, lip gloss, etc. I plan to ask local hairdressers if they can offer coupons for free haircuts. I realize that to provide hundreds of baskets each month on my own will be impossible, but I *can* supply several. The food bank director can then determine which women need more than just their stomachs ministered to. Better yet, perhaps other churches and their members will catch the same vision.

Despair to deodorant to dignity . . . the way to a thankful heart.

You're Okay in My Book

By Edna Bell-Pearson

Most of us cherish the memory of a special person who has influenced our lives in a positive way. My special person was a fellow worker I'll call James Kendall. A deeply religious man who was understanding and sympathetic, James was the most caring person I have ever known. Everybody liked him. His most oft-repeated phrase was, "He (or she) is okay in my book."

"What Lois does out of the office is her business," he'd say. "She's still okay in my book."

Our receptionist's morals were rumored to be somewhat questionable, but James remembered something that the rest of us sometimes forgot—Lois's big heart. It was a rare day when there wasn't a plate of cookies or candy on her desk, and she always remembered to bring in a cake, flowers, or balloons to celebrate a birthday. She went out of her way to do nice things for people, not only in, but out of the office as well.

Lois wasn't the only one who was okay in James's book.

"Joe is okay in my book," he'd say when we complained about Joe Green, a grumpy salesman who no one else in the office liked.

Later, when we learned that Joe's two boys—ages four and six—
were slowly dying from a rare muscular disease, we were more
understanding. Unlike James, however, we had to have a reason
before we could overlook Joe's unpleasant disposition and see him
for the man he truly was.

"People often use anger to hide the way they feel," James said.
"Someone who comes across as irritable or insensitive may actually be suffering—physically, mentally, or emotionally." Also okay
in James's book was Johnny Barton, our delivery boy. We all knew
that Johnny was filching pens, paper, and notepads from the
office. I agreed with the others that he should be fired. That was
before James confided in me that Johnny's dream was to be a
writer. "We shouldn't begrudge him a few supplies," James said.
"His father was laid off several months ago and all of Johnny's
salary goes toward helping to pay the rent and feed a family of
five children."

James was incredibly witty; he could be a lot of fun to be
around. But he always looked for the good in people and I never
heard him say a disparaging word about anyone in all the time
we worked together. His door was always open when we needed
a shoulder to cry on, or someone to listen to our problems. He
honestly seemed to be interested in what we had to say—and to
care. I doubt if there was anyone—from the janitor to the company president—who didn't drop in from time to time "just to
talk."

Because James and I both worked in the communications
department, we saw a lot of each other, and I'm afraid I "bent his
ear" as often as anyone. Like everyone else, I always came away

from his office feeling better. James always seemed to be able to place himself in the other person's shoes. Anytime he saw someone looking sad or worried—at the office, in the elevator, on the street, or in the checkout line at the supermarket—James would stop and strike up a conversation. Almost always, the person walked away wearing a smile. I wished I could be more like James—especially on those occasions when I learned, too late, that I had been so absorbed in my own concerns I overlooked another's need.

It's been years since we went our separate ways, but I still think of James when I find myself being judgmental or overly critical. I try to be more considerate of others.

"What do *you* know about this person—or what he's going through?" I ask myself; and I try a little harder to understand—as James would say—"what makes him tick." James was a tough act to follow, but I'm making progress. This morning when Marge, who lives across the street, called with a bit of gossip about Linda, another neighbor, I thought of the basket of delicious apples Linda had picked for me when she went to the orchard last fall.

"That's her business, Marge," I said. "Besides, do you know anyone more kindhearted than Linda?"

"Well—no," she replied.

Thinking of James, I added, "I don't care what Linda did, or didn't do, she's okay in my book."

Baskets of Blessings

By Cynthia Stiverson

The family's first visit was Easter Sunday in 2006, six months after the launching of our church. Just two days before, on Good Friday, several of us went door-to-door delivering Easter "Baskets of Blessings" to neighboring families. The beautiful baskets were loaded with everything needed for an Easter meal, along with stuffed animals and chocolate bunnies for the children. As pastor and church planter, I envisioned welcoming bright and polished young families into our church through this outreach: families that would be a blessing to us, families that could help meet the overwhelming demands of a new church. But God had a different vision.

It was a single mother, her eight-year-old daughter, and eleven-year-old son who walked through our doors that Sunday. As I talked with her after the service, I learned she was overwhelmed with troubles. She shared that she had divorced her husband after he was convicted and imprisoned for abusing the children. After they left, my children's pastor whispered in my ear, "That is a needy family!" That was quite an understatement. The eleven-year-old had literally screamed nonstop for ten minutes during children's church. We were soon to discover that their needs were overwhelming!

I prayed for the families in my congregation to be faithful in their attendance. How ironic that this particular family would soon rival the attendance of others. Their visit was not limited to that one Sunday. Neither were the episodes of screaming.

The poor boy was totally unapproachable. He would cower in a corner like a wounded animal, his eyes piercing anyone who dared come near. He would not respond when spoken to. We were faced with a real problem. Should we allow one child to disrupt all the others? What if other, *more desirable* young families with children were to visit? Certainly they would not return to this kind of atmosphere. Should we risk turning others away by allowing these children to continue attending? What would be best for growing the church?

As I prayed, I knew our response to this one family was a litmus test that would dictate the future of our church and show our true heart. The easy thing would be to just overlook the family's gaping wounds and dysfunction in hopes they would go away. Instead, we embraced the family and bandaged their wounds.

Some of our men mentored the boy during church. Some provided transportation to enable the family to join our home groups, to help transport them to doctor's appointments, to pick up groceries and prescriptions. Others gave money when the family was low on funds. Our church adopted this family as our Christmas project and filled their home with gifts. Someone donated a car for the mother and the church paid for the necessary repairs. We redecorated and furnished the children's bedrooms and replaced

broken windows in their home. We helped the mother get her
house back in order by cleaning and organizing. One of our college interns who majored in religion and psychology, made weekly
pastoral calls to help the mother establish and enforce house rules.

The change in their lives was amazing! Within a year they were
released from the supervision of children's services. The son's
school grades improved from Ds and Fs to As and Bs. He made
eye contact, engaged in conversation, and allowed us to embrace
him. His mother was quick to put into practice the messages I
had been preaching on evangelism: She invited a total stranger to
church. Her new unchurched friends began attending regularly
as well.

The years have come and gone since that first Easter Sunday.
We've celebrated and grieved with the family in the ups and
downs of their lives. The children have grown physically, spiritually, and emotionally. Both have accepted Christ as their Savior.
He has set them free to enjoy being children. There is life in their
eyes and joy on their faces. They rush to greet everyone with
warm embraces and the latest news. And in just a few weeks, I will
be officiating over their mother's wedding. The children are
elated at the prospect of becoming a family and having a Christian father.

As visitors come and go through the doors of our new church,
it seems the ones we are most hopeful will return, never do. Those
who challenge us the most just kept coming. I suppose that is
God's way of reminding us that the church doesn't exist to meet
its own needs. It exists to meet the needs of others.

One of the most profound statements I've ever heard was that first year at our ladies' retreat. A younger woman turned to this single mother and said, "You bring so much to our church." When we delivered a Basket of Blessings to her home that first year, we had no idea the blessings we would receive in return. The joy of watching God's love transform *their* lives has transformed *our* lives as well.

It's All About Grace

By Elaine L. Bridge

"I'm not going to do it."

I'd made a simple request, and I must admit he gave a straightforward answer. In the throes of teenage rebellion, my son seemed lately to challenge most directives from his parents. Anxious that we refocus on regular devotional times as we entered the new year, I'd asked him to turn off the TV and computer at a certain hour and spend some time with his Bible and his God.

At first it looked like he was going to do so. I was pleasantly surprised, it's true. Mentally I planned to reward his cooperation with the gift of a brand-name T-shirt I knew he wanted. Before I could do so, however, he'd changed his mind and responded defiantly that he wasn't about to do as I'd asked. He stated his reasons and defended them vociferously until I tired of arguing with him. His refusal to do *his* Bible study time was clearly interfering with my attempts to do *mine*. He gave in at last but stomped off in anger, clearly in no mood to glean much spiritually from the effort.

"Well, I'm surely not going to give it to him *now* . . ." I muttered to myself. The wisdom of the world and that of most psychologists states that bad behavior should never be rewarded, and that only positive actions should be reinforced with appropriate treats. But the Bible tells us that we don't think or act like God does, and clearly God had a different opinion on this matter than I did. In fact, He told me to go bless my son with the shirt he wanted at the very moment in which he was the least deserving of it. Unwilling as I was to comply with the order, God had to remind me that *He* gave *me* the greatest blessing of my life when my actions likewise merited it the least. He, too, gave me new clothes to wear—garments of righteousness to replace the sin-soiled rags I was wearing at the time. My deeds demanded the eternal torment of hell, not the everlasting life He offered to me as a gift instead.

I've noticed that God never loses an argument. And He didn't in this instance, either. I headed for my son's room, wrinkling the shirt in my tightly clenched fist and continuing the argument to myself under my breath. I stopped in the doorway only to find my boy lying on his bed with his eyes closed, his Bible lying unopened on the floor several feet away.

"See, God? He's *still* not obeying me," I whispered to Him, certain that He would see things my way at last and change His mind on the matter. But my son's unworthiness seemed only to increase God's determination to bless him, and He gave me the terse order to do it *now*.

And so I shook out the shirt and held it up in front of a pair of disbelieving eyes. I asked my teenager if he still wanted the item. His shocked expression as he reached for it convinced me that God was right once more. In fact, I was amazed to see that my son's heart was changed in an instant. The punishments I'd intended in response to his defiance could never have accomplished that. They might have changed his outward actions, but would have failed to reach the heart inside.

I reaped the benefits of the action that seemed so crazy to me at the time. I was hugged and thanked. He apologized for his earlier behavior, and later even went so far as to gather the dirty dishes and empty pop cans scattered around his room and carry them to the kitchen sink! But what blessed me the most as I went back upstairs was the sight of him picking up his Bible to actually read it. Not that either of us needed to study any more that night. God had just taught *both* of us a lesson on grace.

It All Depends on How You Look at It

By Barbara J. Fisher

I was once blind for six weeks. At the time it seemed like an eternity. Strange though it may seem, during that time, I "saw" the people in my life more clearly than ever. My handicap taught me to see with my heart. At the time, I was in a Columbus hospital; I was very scared, very alone, and extremely homesick for my husband and five kids. I am sure the darkness exaggerated those feelings even more. I spent hours, even days, wondering if I would ever see my children again. I spent so much time feeling sorry for myself, and when the nurse announced I was getting a roommate, I was far from excited. Like it or not, my new roommate, Joni, was moved into the bed beside me.

Despite my best efforts to wallow in self-pity, I took an immediate liking to Joni. Her positive attitude cheered me up, and she never complained about her own illness. Joni would often sense my fear and depression and somehow manage to convince me that I was lucky not to be able to see myself in the mirror. I knew my hair was a mess from lying in bed for a week, and that I was puffy from the cortisone IV's; yet Joni could still get me to laugh at her crazy jokes.

When my husband Joe, would come to visit, he would sometimes bring all five kids with him. Can you imagine dressing five kids under the age of six? He said it often took hours to find ten shoes and socks that matched. After they were gone, Joni spent hours telling me what mixture of costumes each one had worn. Then she would read all the little cards they had brought to me, filled with "I love you" and "Please get well soon, Mommy." When friends sent fresh flowers, she described them to me. She would open my mail and tell me how lucky I was to have so many friends. At mealtime she would help me to find my mouth with the food. She convinced me that, just for the moment, perhaps I was lucky that I couldn't see the hospital food!

One evening Joe came alone. Joni must have sensed our need to be alone. She was so quiet I wasn't sure she was in the room. During his visit, Joe and I talked about the possibility that I might never see again. He assured me that nothing could change his love for me, and that somehow, no matter what, we would always have each other. Together we would continue to raise our family. For hours he just held me in his arms, let me cry, and tried to make my dark world a tiny bit brighter.

After he left, I heard Joni stirring in her bed. When I asked her if she was awake, she said, "Do you know how lucky you are to have so many people loving you? Your husband and kids are beautiful! You are so lucky!"

At that moment, I realized for the first time that during our weeks together in the hospital, Joni never had a husband or child visit. Her mother and her minister came occasionally, but they only stayed a very short time. How selfish I had been! I had been

so wrapped up in myself I hadn't even allowed her to confide in
me. I knew she was very sick, but I didn't even know with what.
Once, I heard her doctor call her illness by a long Latin name, but
I had never asked what it meant. I hadn't even taken the time to
inquire. I hated myself for how selfish I had become.

I turned over and started to cry. I asked God to forgive me. I
promised Him that the first thing the next morning, I would ask
Joni about her illness, and I'd let her know how grateful I was to
her for her unconditional love. I'd tell her that I loved her, too.

I never got the chance. When I awoke the next morning, the
curtain was drawn between our beds. I could hear people whis-
pering nearby. I strained to listen. Then I heard a minister say,
"May she rest in eternal peace." Before I could tell her I loved
her, Joni had died.

I learned later that Joni had come to the hospital for that very
reason. She knew when she was admitted she would never return
home. Yet she had never complained, and had spent the final days
of her life giving hope to me. Joni must have sensed her life was
ending that last night when she told me how lucky I was. After I
had cried myself to sleep, she had written me a note. The nurse
read it to me that morning.

My friend,

*Thank you for making my last days so special! I found great happi-
ness in our friendship. I know that you care for me, too, "sight unseen."
Sometimes to get our full attention, God must knock us down, or at
least make us blind. With my final breath, I pray that you will soon be
seeing again, but not especially in the way you think. If you can only*

learn to see with your heart, then your life will be complete. Remember me with love,

Joni

That night as I lay in bed, I realized for the first time that I could vaguely see the brightness of the tiny night light along the baseboard. My vision was coming back! Only a little bit, but I could see! Even more important, for the first time in my life I could also see with my heart.

I know that Joni was placed in my life for that reason. Even though I never knew what she looked like, I am sure she was one of the most beautiful people in the world.

I have lost my vision several times since her passing, but thanks to Joni I will never allow myself to "lose sight" of the important things in life. Things like warmth, love, and sometimes even sorrow, if shared with someone special, can be beautiful. It all depends on "how you look at it."

The Power of
Prayer

Hair Color 101

By Mimi Greenwood Knight

At some time in their lives, most women will survive a hair-color disaster. I don't know how I avoided it for forty-five years. But last week I found myself planted in front of the bathroom mirror gaping at my reflection with *I Love Lucy* orange hair and not a spare moment on my calendar to slink shame-faced to my hairdresser and beg her to fix it. Even if I could, there wasn't money in my checking account to pay for it. It was one of those months where every nickel is spoken for. That's why I'd attempted the home job in the first place. How could I be so stupid? A frizzy home perm when I was twelve was one thing. Halloween hair at forty-five was another.

To make matters worse, we were in the middle of a drama project at church and I was one of the directors. For the next three nights, 150 church members would gather to reenact the life of Christ for an audience of about 4,000. It's a high point of the year for our church family and I wasn't going to miss it, but I knew my circus-clown hair and I were in for a humbling three days.

Less than an hour after this episode, I was due to speak to my son's third-grade class about being a freelance writer, something

I'd been looking forward to for weeks. I should have called and rescheduled but I drove on to school. My Crayola orange hair and I skulked into the classroom. I wish I had a Polaroid of the look on the face of my son, Hewson.

"Mom!" was all he could manage.

"It was an accident, honey. Don't worry. I can fix it."

"Mom, how do you *accidentally* dye your hair?"

"I'm not sure. But it'll be gone before you know it."

The rest of the class thought it was great (yeah—great that I wasn't their mom). Because they were learning about elections, one student suggested they take a vote, "Who likes Hewson's mom's hair?" Everyone but Hewson flailed both hands in the air. One future politician added, "Actually I like it both ways—brown and pink!" (Hey, this is orange!) Hewson just sat there shaking his head.

I made it through the speech, then started dreading the moment I'd see my twelve- and fourteen-year-old daughters—or rather, the moment they'd see me. Haley was speechless. Molly kept repeating, "Mom, do you really understand how *bad* that looks?" Only three hours until my husband would be home. I could hardly wait! He was actually pretty kind although I did catch him snickering with the kids behind my back.

Now, it was time to go to church. *Lord,* I prayed on the way there, *am I in need of some serious humbling? Is that what this is about? Have I been too big for my britches lately?* The answer, I realized, was *yes.* Pride is a tricky business. It sneaks up on you like the date of your next mammogram. You're going along doing your own thing, then *wham,* it hits you. As my Sunday school teacher once said, "You can become proud of how humble you are." And it's hard to pray and ask God for humility, once you realize you need it, because how do you become humble? By being humiliated—like showing up in a room full of your peers with Tang-colored hair.

Getting out of my car at church, I thought about a time in high school when I used an artificial tanning solution that turned my skin this exact shade of orange and how hard it was walking into the classroom the next day to a barrage of questions from my classmates. Adults are a bit more subtle. The worst I got at church was puzzled looks that seemed to say, "You reckon she *meant* to do that?" I'd be talking to someone, giving him instructions for his costume or props, and catch his eyes wandering up to my hair, then darting back down to my face, bewildered.

Lucky for me, women in Jesus' day had to cover their heads. I couldn't get into my costume fast enough. Maybe I could forget to take it off until everyone was gone. Even my hairdresser was there. When we got a moment alone, I pulled her aside, sheepishly removed my head scarf, and braced myself.

"It's not that bad," she assured me. But three minutes later she added, "Okay it *is* that bad, but we can fix it. Come see me tomorrow." I didn't know how to tell her I couldn't come because I didn't have the money to pay her. *Please Lord, how much humbling do I need?* That's when my son pulled his friend over and said, "See! I told you. Bright orange!" (*Am I there yet, Lord?*)

But the worst was yet to come. Before we all went home for the night, my hairdresser hugged me good-night and whispered in my ear, "When you come in tomorrow, your hair is my treat." I protested but she gave me a look that said, "This conversation is over." *How humble can one person get in twenty-four hours, Lord? Now I'm a charity case.* The next day I showed up for my freebie hair color. It was awkward. It was embarrassing. It was probably just what this prideful Christian needed.

When I returned home with brown hair again plus a terrific new haircut to boot, I looked up *humble* in my Bible reference guide. I found that 1 Peter 5:5 says, "God resists the proud but gives grace to the humble." Luke 14:11 reads, "He who exalts himself shall be humbled but he who humbles himself shall be exalted." And Micah 6:8 says, "What does the Lord require of you but to do justly and to love mercy and to walk humbly with your God?" Maybe humility was exactly what the doctor ordered.

The saga of the orange hair is just a chapter in our family book now. I don't think I'll risk coloring my own hair ever again, and I'm trying to keep pride at bay one day at a time. However, I was in the drug store the other day and saw the self-tanning lotions on discount. I'm considering giving it a shot. I wonder if anyone will notice.

A Special Prayer

By Michael Jordan Segal

My father is the most unselfish person I know—always thinking of others first before thinking of himself. Perhaps that is why he chose to be a rabbi, to serve God by helping other people.

Every Christmas my father, Rabbi Jack Segal, volunteers at a hospital in Houston so that Christian employees can spend the holy day with their loved ones. One specific Christmas, my father was working the telephone switchboard at the hospital, answering basic questions and transferring phone calls. One of the calls he received that day was from a woman who was obviously upset.

"Sir, I understand my nephew was in a terrible car accident this morning. Please tell me how he is."

After the woman gave the boy's name, my father checked the computer and said, "Your nephew is listed in critical condition. I'm truly sorry. I hope he'll get better." As soon as my father said "critical" the woman immediately began to sob and then she screamed, "Oh my God! What should I *do*? What *can* I do?"

Hearing those words, my father the Rabbi stated softly, "Prayer might be helpful at this time."

The woman replied, "Yes—oh, yes. But it's been ten years since I've been to a church and I've forgotten how to pray. Sir, do *you* know how to pray? Could *you* say a prayer for me while I listen on the phone?"

My father quickly answered, "Of course," and began saying the ancient prayer for healing in Hebrew, the *Mee Shebayroch*. He ended the prayer with, "Amen!"

"Thank you, thank you so much," the woman on the phone replied after hearing my father's "Amen." Then she added, "I truly appreciate your prayer, but I have one major problem. I did not understand the prayer, since I do not speak Spanish."

My father chuckled inside and said, "Ma'am, that was not Spanish. I'm a rabbi and that prayer was in Hebrew." The woman gave a sigh of relief and said, "Hebrew? Hebrew? That's great. That's God's language. Now He won't need a translator!"

He Restores My Soul

By Susan Dollyhigh

Driving up the steep, curvy gravel road, I asked the Lord to meet me on the mountain. After a season of intense trial, I needed time alone and the peace and comfort and restoration that can come only through Him.

After breaking my right foot in early spring, I'd been unable to walk or drive for ten weeks. As my world shrunk to four walls, the days crawled by. Satan didn't waste this opportunity, this time of weakness and discouragement, to attack. Life delivered another blow when a crisis arose in my marriage that threatened to break my spirit, my very soul. Each time I returned to the doctor for check-ups and X-rays, the news was the same.

"Why aren't your bones healing?" the doctor finally asked, as if I were the doctor and he the patient. I shrugged as if I didn't know, but inside I suspected the reason had something to do with my heart.

"Why isn't my heart healing?" I cried out to the Lord. I felt so helpless. I felt so alone. I felt so wounded. The words that usually poured from my heart onto the page ceased. This had never happened to me before. Ten weeks after the fall that broke my foot, I returned to the doctor for yet another X-ray. With the report in hand and a smile on his face, he walked into the room and delivered the wonderful news—the bones had healed. Even though my foot was tender and painful to walk on, I enjoyed every step I took. I enjoyed getting into my car and driving once again.

My foot had been restored. But my broken heart—that was another story. I'd come to realize what went into healing a broken bone: having it set, a cast, crutches, pain pills, and visits to the doctor. It took ten weeks for my broken bones to heal. How long, if ever, would it take my heart, broken by betrayal, to heal? *What will it take to heal my spirit?* I agonized. Reading God's Word? Praying? Believing? Acceptance of what I can't change? Desperately needing to get away, I made a reservation for a few days at Pilot Knob Inn. I merely hoped to find peace and a little restoration, thinking my broken spirit couldn't be repaired in one short weekend. I arrived at the tobacco barn cabin, unpacked my bag, and lay down for a nap.

As I closed my eyes, sleep didn't come—prayers did. I cried out to the Lord and began to feel His mighty presence. The room was dark because the view from the small window was obscured by trees. Suddenly, an intense light forced my eyes open. I hadn't seen any opening in the leaves but God allowed the sun to break through and flood not only my face but my heart. I shielded my face from the bright light and felt that I, like Moses, had seen the goodness of the Lord pass by me. *What will it take to heal my spirit?* I'd agonized. The answers that came to me were exactly what the Lord would have me do. Throughout the weekend, I was drawn to God's word and read Scripture that I'd highlighted while going through previous trials. I read all the verses I could find pertaining to healing. I prayed as the Lord continued to turn each nap time into prayer time. I came to believe in a way that I never had before in the mighty power and sustaining grace of our Savior. And I came to understand that I must accept what I cannot change. As I packed my car to return home, I realized how little faith I'd had in our God. I'd asked the Lord to meet me on the mountain and He had done so. I asked him for a little peace and restoration. God gave me His peace and healed my broken spirit. I returned home to the same marital problems I'd left behind, only now, by His grace, I knew I could handle them. The Lord restored my soul.

PG-Rated Prayer

By Teresa Hoy

I walked the darkened neighborhood streets. Except for the usual background hum of the city, quiet enveloped me. It was the same route I had taken the last few Saturday nights. As I walked, my thoughts turned to the Bible study I had begun attending several weeks earlier. The words our teacher had spoken last week had started me thinking differently about prayer. "Be specific when you pray," he had said.

"But God knows what I need already. Why do I have to spell it out in detail?" someone in the group asked. The same question had surfaced in my mind.

He answered, "God knows what you need, but He wants you to ask Him for it. You build a personal relationship with Him that way." He went on to explain that when he and his wife first came to the area, they drove around looking for a house to buy. They decided to ask God to help them find the right house. Praying aloud, they began listing things they felt would fit their needs.

Shortly afterward, they found a house in their price range, with a large finished area in the basement (perfect for Bible study groups) and other features they had mentioned in their prayer. I was amazed by how specific they had been, mentioning all types of details I would never have thought God would want to hear.

I had never prayed too specifically about things. My prayers were more the general kind. *Please bless my family and friends, give me patience, kindness, generosity, and thanks for everything-*type prayers.

As a young single woman, I was hoping to meet a man with whom to share my life. I decided to pray about it, and this time I would be specific. I ambled down the dimly lit sidewalks of my neighborhood praying in detail.

"God," I said, "I want a man who likes to be with family, likes camping, and the outdoors. I want him to like animals. He doesn't have to be a knockout as long as I think he's handsome." I paused. "Oh yeah, I want him to drive a pickup truck."

I'm not sure why I added that last item. I was a country girl who had moved to the city. I guess I associated men who drove pickups with the strong, nature-loving, family man I wanted. The list wasn't perfect, but it was my first time at any kind of specific praying. Anyway, that was my list, and I prayed it repeatedly, always ending with, "If it be Thy will."

A short time passed and I still hadn't met Mr. Right. I dated a guy or two, but they always fell short on at least one of the qualifying factors on my list. Had I been too specific? I decided I must have been and forgot about my detailed prayer until one weekend that summer.

The annual air show was taking place at Richards-Gebaur Air Base in Belton, Missouri. A friend and I decided to go, along with thousands of other aviation enthusiasts. The sun pounded down on us as we wandered the concrete pavement. It was while standing covered in perspiration, heat sucking the breath from me, and a lightheaded wooziness trying to overcome me, that I met Bill. He flew the KC 135 refueling plane for the Air National Guard out of Topeka, Kansas.

I couldn't believe it when he offered to show me around the plane. He not only gave me a tour of the plane but also asked my friend and me to join him and his crewmembers on the huge wing of the plane, a great vantage point for watching the air show.

Bill was tall, blond, and blue-eyed. He was kind and personable. However, if he was Mr. Right, it was too early to tell. He took my phone number and flew back to Topeka. He told me before leaving that he worked in Topeka but lived in Missouri, north of the river, not too far from where I lived.

I worked nights, operating the mainframe computer for a large real estate company. One night the following week, I received a phone call from Bill. We talked about how our weeks were going, and then he asked me out for Saturday night. I agreed to go.

Before he hung up he said, "There's just one thing."

"Yes?"

"I only drive a pickup truck."

My jaw dropped.

"That's okay," I said calmly while my insides flip-flopped.

Over the next weeks and months, I met Bill's dog, spent a lot of time with his family, took him camping and boating with my family, and eventually married him.

As time passed, I began to realize God had not only answered my prayer, but He had also given me much more than I had asked for.

Generosity, compassion, intelligence, and love were things I had forgotten to put on that list, but God gave me a man with all of those qualities.

That happened many years ago, but I remember it vividly to this day. That experience changed my view of God. I had always believed God took care of big issues, but I thought of Him somewhere in the distance, out there in the universe taking care of more important business than my personal needs. Now, I had felt his touch in the tiniest details of my life.

I remember that feeling when I pray. So, instead of my prayers being G-rated for general, they are now rated PG—for Personal God.

Battle Plans

By Annmarie B. Tait

In early June of 1968, the excitement of school letting out for the summer fizzled in the shadow of my older brother's Army enlistment during the height of the Vietnam War. I was in the fifth grade and the youngest of five children. It was a grim year on the battlefields. So, on the morning of June 12 when Bobby left for Fort Bragg, North Carolina, teary-eyed goodbyes were the featured event. These were not the usual "You're going off on your own and we'll miss you like crazy" sentimental tears, the kind shed for siblings setting out for college dorms, or getting married. These were "Oh my gosh, this is war and you could wind up dead!" kinds of sobs validated by gruesome nightly newsreels and morbid photos spread over the pages of *Life* magazine.

As we sobbed and sighed, Mom stood her ground and never shed a tear, at least none that I ever saw. My mother was no stranger to the fear that war imparts. Mom was a World War II veteran herself; she'd enlisted with the first class of U.S. Marine Corps Women's Reserves in 1943. "Free a Man to Fight" was the poster slogan that drew her to the recruiting office. Against her own mother's wishes, she followed her heart and enlisted for love of country. In those days, military regulations prevented women from battle but she had a front-row seat to the aftermath and tragedy that war inflicted on one family after another. Even with her background and experience she stood stoic with full faith that Bobby would return home unharmed. Her military training was not the well from which she drew her strength: Mom's faith was invested in a higher authority. Like any good Marine she had a battle plan. The rest of us had the reality of Walter Cronkite's nightly casualty count, which hit far too close to home for us every time we heard about another neighborhood kid who would never return home to dribble a basketball.

That evening as we ate dinner, we did our best to ignore the empty seat at the table. Just the night before my six-foot five-inch clown of a brother had been there, hurling remarks at his four sisters in his usual wisecracking style. Now in somber silence we toyed with the food on our plates until Mom began clearing the table.

Just as we headed out of the kitchen to study for final exams, my mother ordered an "about face." We turned on our heels and walked back in. With very little fanfare she pulled her old wooden rosary beads out of her apron pocket and promptly announced that we would say the rosary together every night for the duration of Bobby's boot camp. We would say the rosary and pray that God would spare my brother from active duty in Vietnam. In return, God would hear and answer our prayers. Of this she had absolutely no doubt. Right then and there I was sure my mother had officially lost her mind. I knew of no one from our neighborhood who had enlisted and escaped Vietnam—*no one.* And, excuse me, but did she really think I was going to kneel down on the cold, hard kitchen floor for a half hour every night for the next twelve weeks to say the rosary . . . *out loud?* What if my friends walked by and heard us? It wasn't cool. Concern for my brother was one thing, but I didn't see the need to turn into religious fanatics. But Mom had a plan and it was clear from the look on her face that I had no choice.

So the first night of my brother's enlistment we all knelt together in the kitchen on the cold, hard floor and recited the rosary. Then we did it the next night, and the next, until one day in September when my brother called right after his boot-camp graduation ceremony to tell Mother he had his orders. He called at dinnertime so we were all close at hand. Mom answered—it was the first time she'd heard his voice since he'd left home—and she beamed. The call didn't last more than a minute or two.

"Yes, yes . . . I'll tell them right away . . . take care of yourself . . . bye-bye." *Click.* She hung up the phone and for the first time since my brother left, Mom cried. We said the rosary again that night, but this time we said it in thanksgiving. My brother's entire platoon was headed for Vietnam—with the exception of two recruits. Bobby and one other private had been selected for special duty in northern Italy. Bobby spent the duration of his enlistment there.

Such was the faith my mother had in the Lord. She never wavered for one moment when it came to seeking a miracle, no matter the odds. She was relentless with prayer. Sometimes I think God gave in just so she would change the subject! My mother was a Marine with a battle plan—a plan that usually started with her old wooden rosary beads.

Someone to Talk To

By Alyssa Fanara

I have gone to St. Luke's Church for as long as I can remember.
That was where I had my preschool classes, baptism, the
overnight retreat and communion. When I was ten or eleven, I
stopped going to Sunday school and started going with my parents
to the service. When I was twelve, I started to pay attention in
church and to our pastor, Dr. Kent Millard. I was amazed by his
sermons. He is an absolutely amazing speaker, and I loved how
he threw in jokes and stories. Each sermon he spoke had an
important message within it as well.

When I turned thirteen, everything started changing. My nana,
who I love with all my heart, broke her hip. I felt so nervous going
to the hospital to see her. My two lifelong best friends and I got
into a terrible fight, and junior high became a shark tank. On top
of this, there was a family issue that came so suddenly I didn't
know what hit me. I felt like the safe, secure world I had as a child
was falling apart. I began to worry. I worried about almost everything going on at the time. Nighttime was the only opportunity I
had to think to myself. Some nights I'd stay up worrying and sometimes crying until long past the time I was supposed to go to sleep.

I wasn't sure who to talk to. I had my friends (when they weren't backstabbing each other). I also had a therapist and obviously I had my parents, but it wasn't enough. I needed someone else; I needed someone outside of all this. I wanted someone that I wasn't afraid to confess everything to.

One night I came up with the perfect person. Now, I had never been an extremely religious person, although I believed in God, went to church, listened to the sermons, and took communion. I never prayed in the morning or before I went to bed. I had nothing against praying; I had just never done it. However, that one night I decided I was going to try it.

I was all alone in my room and I prayed to God. I confessed all my worries and fears and told Him exactly what I felt without holding back or editing out details. I didn't worry about what He would think or how I'd feel afterward. It was all honesty. I had heard that praying should be built on thanks and gratitude rather than asking for things, but I was desperate. I asked what I should do and admitted that I needed help or advice or anything to help me survive the year. I never got completely through my prayer because I went to sleep earlier than I had in my worrying days.

The following Sunday I went with my parents to church. It was a habit for me so I woke up early, got dressed, and was half asleep in the car ride there. We arrived and I was looking through the program when the title of the sermon caught my eye: "The Antidote to Worry."

That was the most stunned I had ever been in my life. I suddenly felt a wave of relief and shock, but in the most amazing way. He had heard me and listened to me and that alone was enough to make me have faith. I listened very closely to the pastor, and my spirit lifted. I ended my worries and began to see the bright side of everything.

I am now fourteen and my family is stronger than before, my nana is doing well, and my best friends and I are still close. My pastor changed my view of life, and I'm forever grateful.

Mysterious and Wonderful Prayer

By Jerry Hendrick

Prayer is a mysterious thing. As a Christian I have believed in it for as long as I can remember, but I haven't engaged in it nearly as much as I feel I should. It seems like the idea to pray often comes to me (and to many of my Christian friends) as more of an afterthought when "Plan A" doesn't work. Some even see it as little more than a brief ritualistic practice to take part in at certain moments of our day and week.

Most of us pray before we eat, simply because this is what we were taught when we were young. We also pray before we go to sleep, and even if we have graduated beyond the memorized "Now I lay me down to sleep . . ." version, it often seems like more of a habit than anything else. Sundays tend to have their own unique, even more intense, prayer traditions for those of us who attend church. Depending on where we worship, we know the specific times we are "supposed" to pray. We pray at the beginning of the service, just before the offering is taken, and after the sermon is over and we are about to be sent home. We have all learned that these are the appropriate times set aside for prayer, and these expectations have become wired into our inner-prayer psyches.

When I think about my own life as a believer and the role that prayer has played in my walk with God, my memory begins when I was a middle-school-aged boy asking Jesus to forgive me of my sins. This prayer happened toward the end of a particularly moving evening service when I felt a need for God like I had never felt before. It was an intense and emotional time for me, and as I look back on it today, I believe this was when I took my first intentional step toward a life of love and service of Him.

There was another intense prayer period that lasted several weeks when I was fifteen and was certain that I had already "fallen in love" with the beautiful girl who walked into the choir room of our high school on that first day of school. In the days and weeks that followed, I pursued Beth with unbelievable (and incredibly annoying) persistence, and spent my last moments awake every night praying to God to "make" her love me back. I don't remember everything I said to God during those emotional late-night prayers, but I do remember that I did a lot of bargaining. "God, if you will make Beth love me then I will promise to always love and serve You." I made countless promises of this type before Beth finally relented to my persistence, and while I must confess to being a little embarrassed today about the nature of those prayers, it does help to know that they were the prayers of a young, immature, and infatuated male. It also helps to reflect on the fact that Beth did end up loving me, and we have now been married for more than twenty-two years.

There is one other period of intense prayer of my more than thirty years of life as a Christ-follower. This period was the ten months that our family spent involved with my daughter's cancer. I have never prayed more intensely than during that time, and I have never been more focused on the importance of my prayers and the prayers of others for her. I am convinced that it is because of these prayers that she is still with us today; living, laughing, and loving God as only she can.

There are many things I do not understand about prayer. I have read and listened to others' attempts at explanation, but the truth is I am a little skeptical of what I hear them say. My own thought is that God is far too great for us to understand Him and His ways, and I think that prayer is a part of this incredible mystery. What I do know, based on what I have experienced in life, is that prayer really does work; not always in the way we want it to, but it works nonetheless. If we go to God with a pure heart in prayer, He will listen and answer in His time and manner.

I wrote the following prayer after asking God for direction in the areas of my life where I most need His help. It is my prayer, and while there may be parts in it that are also relevant to you, it was not written with the purpose of being equally applicable to all. My prayer is personal, and it applies in a most personal way to the areas I feel God wants me to develop and grow in my own walk with Him. In a similar way, you must ask God for guidance in the areas where you need His help. I think that prayers of this nature play an important role in our never-ending need for continued spiritual growth. I will pray that God reveals to you the areas of your own life where you need His help.

My Prayer
God grant me a thankful heart, so I appreciate all of the blessings I have been given.

God grant me strength, so I can stand up to whatever trials I will face in life.

God grant me courage, so I will live a fearless life for You.

God grant me grace, so I will accept without complaint whatever comes my way.

God grant me faith, so I will stay true when doubt and discouragement attack my spirit.

God grant me compassion, so I might show Your love toward others; near and far.

God grant me humility, so I will remember I am no better than anyone else.

God grant me character, so I might be an example for others.

God grant me patience, so I am able to wait for Your perfect timing.

God grant me forgiveness, so I can forget whatever wrongs I have known.

God grant me love, so that I might warm Your heart and the souls of those I meet.

God grant me peace, that only comes from pleasing You.

Must-Know Info

Must-Know Info

Miracles Big and Small

By J. Brent Bill

"It's a miracle!" I've been heard to shout that on a sub-zero day when my long driveway was shut with drifting snow, and I got the tractor started. But I didn't really mean it was a miracle. What I meant was I was surprised that the tractor started.

That's one way many of us use the word miracle: to describe something good happening unexpectedly.

Of course, the other way is when something truly miraculous happens, such as when a friend who had deadly cancer not only survives but is declared in remission—and remains healthy for years.

Still, both make me wonder about miracles, big and small. Are miracles of many sizes occurring around us all the time? Do we miss them because we don't really expect miracles as part of our mostly rational everyday life?

When we read the Bible, we come face to face with miracles. They pop up all the time, it seems, from blind men receiving sight, to sick women being healed, to water turning into wine. So what's different today? It's the way we look at life. We move through it so fast and with such little attention that we often miss the good graces of God that are present all around us all the time. If that is so, then do we learn to see miracles?

The answer, I believe, is learning to "pay attention in love." Paying attention in love is an idea I first encountered in the writing of Belden C. Lane, Ph.D., of St. Louis University.

Lane believes that paying attention in love allows anything, even ordinary things, to become a way of glimpsing the profound. He quotes the Psalmist as asking, "Hither shall I go from thy Spirit? Or whither shall I flee from thy presence?" and responds, in essence, "There's nowhere, God is everywhere." Once we focus our attention in love on the holy ordinary, Lane maintains, it's hard for us to ever again see the people and things around us as anything but gifts from God. Our lives then no longer move between the two camps of the secular and the sacred—*all* is sacred.

Paying attention in love enables us to stop and see the miracles present in everyday life. Paying attention in love shows us that the poetry of the Psalms is *more* than poetry—"Then the trees of the forest will sing, they will sing for joy before the Lord, . . . Give thanks to the Lord, for he is good; his love endures forever."

Singing trees and jubilant fields are poetic, to be sure. But perhaps the words the Psalmists use are more than metaphor— perhaps they point to miracles. I have seen the golden light of autumn transform a field of corn stubble into something that is jubilant while subtle—a light that reflects God's light. Likewise, by paying attention in love, it is easy for me to see the naked brown-black winter limbs of the trees in the woods next to my house as hands uplifted in praise to God.

An appreciation for the divinely mysterious presence of God
helps us see the miracles all around us. The Divine mark rests
upon all of life's goodness. Learning to see miracles speaks to my
heart and reminds me that everything is a miracle. Appreciat-
ing that everything is a miracle leads us into a new way of seeing the hand of God in all with which we have been blessed. We
see that every moment is miraculous, filled with the presence of
God.

I think that's why an English Quaker named William Little-
boy once wrote:

> God is above all the God of the normal. In the common facts and
> circumstances of life, He draws near to us, quietly. He teaches us in
> the routine of life's trifles, gently, and unnoticed. His guidance comes
> to us through the channels of "reason [and] judgment". . . we have
> been taught by Him when we least suspected it; we have been
> guided . . . though the guiding hand rested upon us so lightly that we
> were unaware of its touch.

So how do we learn to see these everyday miracles around us?
Here are three tips you might find helpful.

Stop and take a breath. Yes, physically stop whatever you're
doing, take a deep breath, and while you're exhaling slowly, take
a look around. What captures your attention? Where is the
miracle in what you're seeing?

Look with playful eyes. The poet Gerald Manley Hopkins
wrote that "Christ plays in ten thousand places. . . ." Where do
you think Christ might be playing around you?

Listen with an open heart. Take some time for silence. And in that silence ask God what miracles He has brought you this day that you need to pay attention to. Take time to listen for God's reply.

Paying attention in love to God's guiding hand resting lightly upon us points us to the miracles around us every day—big and small.

Must-Know Info
Living the Golden Rule
By Dr. Linda McCoy

Jesus said, "Treat others just as
you want to be treated."

—LUKE 6:31

A few years ago, there was an Eagles' song titled, "Hole in the World." This song spoke of those challenging areas of life where we experience an abyss or a dark time. We have all experienced those times in life when it does seem as though there is a hole in the world: holes of sadness, fear, pain, hatred, prejudice, intolerance, or brokenness.

Both our personal and global relationships are fractured and fragmented. Unbridled anger and unimaginable atrocities go on around us on a daily basis—cruel and inhumane treatment of humans by other humans. I find myself wondering how we can treat one another so cruelly. Why, when we're all imperfect mortals, are we so quick to blast another person? Why do we seemingly have such little regard for others?

Is it that we're filled with some sort of irreconcilable anger? Is it because we are afraid? Is it that we are consumed with hatred— for self and *others*? I'm certainly not an expert on this, but it's clear that these "holes" exist in far too many places in our world.

I have been trying to make some sense of this darkness, and I wonder if maybe part of the problem is our disrespect for the worth and dignity of every human being. We seem to think others aren't as worthy as we are, and so we ignore or persecute them; we're intolerant of those who don't look, act, think, or believe as we do.

The thing that surprises and saddens me is how that very same intolerance and disregard for others exists among some of us who claim to be Christians, who profess to be followers of Jesus. Let me share with you what I mean. Two or three years ago, I was asked to speak to a group of pastors in another state. They were interested in learning about the how's and why's of my ministry, and everything went fairly well until the question and answer time. The questioner asked what I call the litmus test, to determine whether or not I am "Christian." I regret to say that I answered a bit defensively and not very lovingly, and, to put it mildly, an uproar ensued.

I appreciated those who came to me afterward for further discussion, because that gave us the opportunity to share various points of view. However, not everyone took the time to do that. Instead, I received a couple of really hurtful e-mails from some of the Christian pastors in attendance, which caused me to harden my view of those who hold a different theological perspective from my own.

That experience opened my eyes to how quickly intolerance and disrespect can grow, and I realized that I was just as guilty of it as those who disagreed so vehemently with me! I was as intolerant of their views as they were of mine, though both views fit well within the parameters of what it means to be Christian. Religious intolerance is the absence of respect for the fundamental right of other people to hold religious beliefs different from our own, and all parties were guilty that day.

What is a different way to be? Luke's gospel speaks to this when it offers us what is commonly referred to as the Golden Rule. The contemporary version is "Treat others just as you want to be treated." Jesus is the one speaking, but what we may not realize is that Jesus sets forth the Golden Rule in the context of loving our enemies. In fact, this passage begins with the words, "Love your enemies, and be good to everyone who hates you. Ask God to bless anyone who curses you, and pray for everyone who is cruel to you."

Jesus wasn't the only one who taught about ethical living. The Golden Rule has become so prevalent in many religious faiths that it is regarded today as a universal moral truth that is probably best understood as a principle by which we can determine our consistency. Are our actions toward another person or group in or out of harmony with our desires for how we want to be? If we violate the Golden Rule, we are violating the spirit of fairness and concern that lies at the very heart of morality. When we are disrespectful toward another person, we are not acting in accord with the Golden Rule. All too often, we've forgotten, ignored, or failed to recognize another as a child of God, created and loved by God—just like us. By our lack of respect, we are being unfaithful to how God would have us live.

There is a better way to live that's told in a Native American fable. It is the story of a Cherokee teaching his grandson about the battle that raged inside him and all of us. He said, "My son, it is between two wolves. One is evil: anger, envy, sorrow, regret, greed, arrogance, self-pity, guilt, resentment, inferiority, lies, false pride, superiority, and ego. The other is good: joy, peace, love, hope, serenity, humility, kindness, benevolence, empathy, generosity, truth, compassion, and faith."

The grandson thought about it for a minute, and then asked his grandfather, "Which wolf wins?"

The old Cherokee answered simply, "The one I feed."

In order to feed the right one, we need God in our lives—to soften our hearts, to give us the capacity to show empathy and compassion for those who may be different from us. We need God to fill our hearts with love for every human being in this world. May we be filled to overflowing so we can truly love one another and treat everyone the way we want to be treated.

Tips for Living the Golden Rule

- You are not in the other person's skin, so try to be more patient and understanding of his or her actions.
- Try to withhold judgment when encountering someone with a viewpoint different from your own.
- Commit to look for the spark of divinity within each person, and honor it.
- Do at least one small act of kindness every day.
- Ask God for a loving heart and "soft eyes" with which to see your fellow human beings.

Must-Know Info

Ministering to Teenagers

By Kurt Johnston

I spend the vast majority of my time working with junior high school-age youth. As a result, a good portion of my time is spent eating pizza, playing dodgeball, paying for Slurpees at 7-Eleven, and clearing toilet paper from my front yard. What do I do with the rest of my time? I spend it trying to convince other adults to join me; selling them on the idea that eating pizza, playing dodge ball, paying for Slurpees at 7-Eleven, and clearing toilet paper from their front yard may be the greatest Kingdom investment they will ever make.

Since 1997, I have served as the junior high pastor at Saddleback Church in Southern California. I work with a fantastic Senior Pastor who believes in our ministry and has generously provided our youth ministry with plenty of "stuff" (support from the elders, a good budget, a nice youth center, etc.) to build a strong ministry to teenagers. While all the "stuff" is great, and I'm thankful for it, there's something else Pastor Rick Warren has given us that has had the greatest impact of all. Rick understands that people are more important than programs, that a building doesn't make a great church; building people does. Rick has preached, and modeled, the simple philosophy that God usually shows up in people's lives through other people; that inspired preaching, a fantastic facility, exciting programs, and other such "stuff" is pointless if people aren't willing to share life together.

And while this is certainly true for adults, I'm convinced that it's even truer when it comes to teenagers. A while ago while writing some training material for our adult volunteers, I was struggling to articulate the complexities of youth ministry in a way that wouldn't scare our leaders off. As I struggled away, I suddenly had an "ah-ha" moment that has revolutionized both me personally and the ministry I lead.

I came up with a very elaborate formula for successful youth ministry: *Teenager + Caring Adult = Good Stuff!* That's it—yes, I'm serious. I still train my adult leaders, but that formula is where we start. At the end of the day, the best youth ministry happens when adults share life with teenagers. I would even go so far as to say that without this happening, nothing else you are doing really matters.

A few years ago I got a phone call from Pastor Rick. It was early on a Friday afternoon and I had sneaked out of the office a little early to go for an evening surf. The conversation went something like this:

Pastor Rick: "Kurt, this is Rick . . . let's have a party at my house tonight with some junior-highers. I just bought a new pool table and I think you guys should come break it in. Call a bunch of your small group leaders and invite them and their kids to come to my house tonight at 6:00. I'll buy the pizza."

Truth be told, it wasn't much of a conversation. Rick was so excited, so pumped up at the prospect of having a bunch of our kids over to his house that he didn't leave room for me to get a word in. At first I was frustrated. I was on my way to the beach and the idea of abandoning those plans to rally a spontaneous party felt more painful than a shark attack! But the frustration was quickly replaced by this observation: My senior pastor wanted to hang out with a bunch of junior-high kids on a Friday night!

I'm not sure Rick would articulate my fantastically deep formula the way I do, but he certainly understands it: **Teenager + Caring Adult = Good Stuff!** I made a few phone calls, and a few hours later Rick's house was full of junior-high students and their adult leaders partying it up. While Rick downed root-beer floats and demolished seventh-graders in billiards, I sneaked up to his home office and penned the now world-famous first sentence of A *Purpose-Driven Life*. (Okay, that last part's not true, but that would be an awesome story.)

On the surface, our youth ministry looks pretty good. We do a good job of creating programs and activities that are fun and attractive to students; we provide missions trips, ministry teams and leadership opportunities; and we preach God's word faithfully and engagingly. As a result, good things are happening, God is moving, and lives are being changed for eternity. And while I'd like to take the credit for it by pointing to the programs I've created and the wonderful messages I've preached to students (if you believe that one, you obviously have *never* heard me speak!), I can't. The truth is I have created a bunch of really good "surface-level" youth ministry elements, but the good stuff is what is happening below the surface.

You see, it's below the surface that our ministry really shines.

Just below the surface is an incredible team of caring adults who are spending time with students. They lead small groups in their homes, they show up at football games, they eat pizza, play dodge-ball, pay for Slurpees at 7-Eleven, and clear toilet paper from their front yards.

Must-Know Info
Before You Call Your Pastor
By Gaye Clark

When life grows chaotic, a ministry morphs into headaches, or dreams turn into nightmares, call the preacher. I did—and felt slighted by the initial response.

"Dr. George Robertson's first available opening is next month, Gaye. If we need to get you in sooner, perhaps we can arrange a phone call?"

Preferring a face to face, I waited my turn. After all, it gave me more time to pray that the meeting would be helpful. When that day arrived, I made one mistake. I told my husband about the appointment over breakfast.

Jim dropped his fork and looked up with a devilish grin. "We okay? You're not going to report me or something, are you?"

I reached over and squeezed Jim's hand. "It has nothing to do with you. It's my ladies' bible study. These women have huge needs and I have few resources. I just felt the senior pastor ought to know what's going on and lend his support when I need it. I've been waiting weeks to see George."

Jim went back to breakfast. "Uh huh. You know these hash browns are great, honey."

Very clever, Jim Clark. "Uh huh? What do you mean by that?

'Fess up. You don't think meeting with George is a good idea, do you?"

Jim grabbed his napkin and wiped his mouth before he spoke. "I'm not going to talk you out of it, but think on this, sweetheart. What is it you expect the man to do for you?"

Such an obvious question. What were my motives? I gave his question some serious thought. My real wants, once revealed, turned my stomach. I wanted:

1. A pat on the back, even though I might manage to mention in conversation the perfunctory, "My ministry is all *God's* doing, of course."
2. Assurance that the pastor knew more than just my name and I mattered. In a church of over 1,500 people, I often felt anonymous.
3. A means to lighten the load. I felt I had more than I could handle.
4. A real solution—a pastoral answer—to the big questions that my ministry created.

As if his thought-provoking question wasn't enough, Jim hit me with another. "Who's going with you? If you leave his office disenchanted, you need to consider that you won't go down alone. You could take a good friend with you into that disappointment. Great breakfast, honey. I have to go to work."

Faithful are the wounds of a friend *and husband.* His response annoyed me. Still, the man had a point.

I thought of cancelling the appointment. Instead, I went to my prayer closet with my not-so-hidden motives for meeting. That helped me to remember that He had answers, resources, and riches far beyond my ability to count. I should have called Him first.

My second epiphany came as I thought of Diane, my friend and ministry partner. What would encourage her in that brief hour we'd have? Prayer. Nothing else would come close.

I had squandered many prayer times with fifty-five minutes of explanations and five minutes of prayer, and I didn't want to make that mistake again. I went to my computer, filled two pages with prayer requests, and carried three copies of the finished product to the meeting.

When we arrived at the church office, George wasn't there. His secretary explained that he'd been delayed with several meetings running longer than expected.

Diane noticed the big picture right away. "I suppose everyone wants a little piece of his time, and there is only so much time to give. We'll be glad to wait." A few minutes later, George arrived at the office.

He opened the door wide and extended his hand. "Sorry to be late. Come on in, ladies. Good to see you."

As we entered his office, I noticed his next appointment waiting, having arrived early. What must it be like for George to sit and listen to person after person as they ask for recognition, assurance, and relief? Personally, I'd be exhausted by the end of the day.

George gestured toward three chairs in front of his desk, sat down in one of them and leaned forward, and asked what he could do for us. I gave George his copy of my prayer requests and spilled out the speech just as I'd rehearsed.

"Well, George, I had planned to tell you all about the problems Diane and I are having with this ministry. That's when it became obvious that they are too big for you. They're too big for us too. We need to pray. So I typed up some requests."

George turned his attention to the paper. "This is great. Can I keep this? It will help me pray later as well."

I looked hard at Diane as I spoke, hoping she'd forgive the no-warning approach. "Diane and I will start to pray, maybe go back and forth a little, and when you catch up with us by reading and praying, then feel free to join us."

George's perplexed delight seemed obvious to me. He hadn't expected this at all. I secretly thanked the Lord for my husband, the man of hard, but great, questions.

We did talk briefly after praying through the requests, but in a different light than I originally planned. What would praying first, then talking, offer us stiff-necked sheep who often feel insignificant? I think my partner in ministry, Diane Hubbard, knew. She reflected on our meeting later.

"We grow overwhelmed and think we can't do anything unless the pastor holds our hand. It is far more helpful to look at what God has done, is doing, rather than to sit and focus on how impossible the task is. We need to leave impossible tasks at the altar."

George closed the prayer time with these words, "Lord, I thank you for the privilege of praying in the middle of the afternoon for Kingdom-building things with these two women."

As we walked out, the next visitor jumped up and looked anxiously toward the door. It made me wonder, what would happen if we sheep went straight to the top with our needs—to God first—then to the senior pastor if need be? George might find his appointment book a little less demanding.

We often feel slighted or ignored if the senior pastor isn't right there when we call him. We wonder if he truly cares about us, question whether he's a people person and whine about feeling unheard. Meanwhile, note the irony. We bypass the God of all creation on our quest to meet with someone higher up the church "org" chart.

I've never had a more satisfying visit with a pastor than the one on that afternoon. It caused me to think on something George's predecessor, Dr. Ray Ortlund, Jr., said of the pastorate: "My role is to bring you to God and leave you there."

When Meeting with the Pastor Is Not a Good Idea

1. **You want to discuss other people.** If you have a genuine concern for a fellow church member, meet directly with that person, or if necessary, bring him with you to see your pastor. It's the best way to avoid gossip veiled as compassion.

2. **You want to discuss things that just don't matter.** Your needs aren't the only ones that your pastor must respond to. Ask yourself the following questions: Does your concern have eternal significance? Is it essential to the church ministry or your spiritual well-being?

3. **You realize someone else is better suited to help you.**

While it can feel great to spend time with the senior pastor, God has given each member of the body a variety of gifts. Consider whether your needs might be better met by contacting an elder, deacon, or professional counselor.

4. **You want to discuss a problem without offering a solution.** My *own* concerns had no human answers. Before you make the call, ask yourself, "What do I want from my pastor and am I willing to be part of the answer?"

5. **You want to discuss how much you loved or hated the last pastor.** Your current pastor is neither a suggestion box nor a church historian. The previous pastor may have known about your needs and handled them in a way that made you glad/mad/sad but now he's gone. Ask yourself what you want your new pastor to do with this information.

6. **You want to unload something you're tired of carrying.** Most everyone calls the senior pastor out of personal need. Sometimes it's best to carry those needs directly to God. Consider making an appointment with your pastor and when he asks, "What can I do for you?" tell him you are praying for him and want to spend a few minutes asking that God would do something awesome in your church. He just might faint.

Must-Know Info

Faith on the Move

By William H. Willimon

All of the gospels depict Jesus as one who is constantly on a journey. "Follow me!" he called to his first disciples. There was no way to be with Jesus without walking with him.

God promised to come, in spite of our sad human history. God vowed to come out to us, to show us His glory, power, and love. That all sounded good until God Almighty dramatically made good on the promise and actually showed up as Jesus of Nazareth, not the vague and thoroughly adorable God whom we expected. Even among Jesus's closest followers, his twelve disciples, there was this strange attraction to him combined with an odd revulsion for him. "Blessed is the one who takes no offense in me," he said. But the things Jesus said and did led many to despise him. On a dark Friday afternoon in Jerusalem, that revulsion became bloody repulsion as Jesus's hands and feet were nailed to a cross and he was hoisted up naked over a garbage dump outside of town. At last something decisive had been done about Jesus and the God he presented, or so we thought.

Three times Jesus had hinted that his death might not be the end of the drama, yet the thought that anything in the world might be stronger than death was inconceivable to everyone around Jesus, even as it is inconceivable today. First-century near-Eastern primitive people did not know many things that we know, but everybody knew that what's dead stays dead. All of his disciples were quickly resigned to his death; end of story.

But as is so often the case with a true and living God, our sin was not the end of the story. Three days after Jesus had been brutally tortured to death by the government—egged on by a consortium of religious leaders, deserted by his disciples, and then entombed—a couple of his female followers went out in the early morning darkness to the cemetery. The women ventured forth, despite the risk in the predawn darkness, to pay their last respects to the one who had publicly suffered the most ignominious of deaths.

At the cemetery, place of rest and peace for the dead, the earth quaked. The huge stone placed by the soldiers before the entrance (why on earth would the army need a big rock in front of a tomb to keep in the dead?) was rolled away. An angel, messenger of God, was perched impudently upon the rock. The angel preached the first Easter sermon: "Don't be afraid. You seek Jesus, who was crucified? He is risen. Come, look at where he once lay in the tomb." Then the angel commissioned the women to become Jesus's first preachers: "Go, tell the men that he has already gone back to Galilee. There you will meet him."

It was a typically Jesus sort of moment, with people thinking they were coming close to where Jesus was resting only to be told to go somewhere else. Jesus is God in motion: on the road, constantly going somewhere, often to where he is not invited. Jesus was warned by his disciples not to go to Jerusalem, but ever the bold traveler, he had not let danger deter him. And now, on the first Easter morning, death could not daunt his peripatetic mission. Jesus was once again on the move. So in effect, the angel said to the women, "You're looking for Jesus? Sorry, just missed him. If you are going to be with Jesus, you had better get moving!"

The spiritual life based upon a relationship with a living God means a life on the move. If you are going to worship Jesus in word and deed, then you had better be prepared to relocate. Let's get going.

Must-Know Info
Facing Challenges in Your Life
By Todd Outcalt

In the summer of 1999, I organized a large group from our congregation to go to the RCA Dome in Indianapolis to hear Reverend Billy Graham speak. That appearance would turn out to be his final visit to Indiana. Dr. Graham, of course, was an icon to many, and most people—young and old alike—were excited to be attending a Billy Graham crusade.

That evening Billy Graham was escorted onto the stage to wild and thunderous applause. He walked unsteadily, cane in hand, and when he took hold of the pulpit there was a noticeable tremor in his arms. And yet his voice and his testimony were steady and strong. During his introduction, he talked about his wife, Ruth, who was ill, and offered up some insights into his own family. Finally, he talked briefly about his ongoing struggle with Parkinson's disease and the challenges it presented.

As I listened to Dr. Graham that night, I pondered God's strength in the midst of our weakness, and felt an amazing rush of grace. As Billy Graham talked about his own challenges, everyone in the dome that night also considered their own obstacles, setbacks, and needs—and thought about how God might provide an answer to prayer.

Little did I know how much Dr. Graham's sermon that evening would address some of the challenges in my own family, when, some months later, my wife was diagnosed with breast cancer.

Her cancer diagnosis was, by far, the greatest challenge we have had to overcome. There was information to obtain, doctors to consult, decisions to be made. Over the span of two intense weeks, my wife read books, pamphlets, websites, and articles about her particular form of breast cancer. We prayed, and we asked others to pray, too. And in the end, we set our hope in God and for complete healing and wholeness.

God provided.

Often, the largest challenges we face prove to be the biggest proofs we get of God's strength and love. When we have reached the end of our rope is when God throws us a lifeline. The Bible is replete with stories of God helping the weak in time of need; stories about people who faced enormous obstacles but were able to overcome with God's guidance and help.

Take Abraham and Sarah, for instance. This old couple was instructed to leave their native land and take up residence in a new land, and they were promised a family to boot. Talk about doing the impossible! Or how about young David and his giant, Goliath? It only took a small stone and a dose of faith for David to overcome. Or how about Peter, who overcame a lack of faith and a denial? Even Paul had his weaknesses, and came to the conclusion that God's grace was sufficient.

Each of us has challenges in our lives. We are never perfected, complete, or so all-together that we can find everything we need inside ourselves and our own abilities. Even as people of faith, we often discover that our path is littered with thorns, or that we must jump many mud puddles, or that the path is not clearly marked. Life is not always easy. We wish it was, but nothing of value ever falls into our lives without struggle, sacrifice, or desire.

Consider your struggles. What challenges are you facing? Don't give in . . . look up. God is near and will come swiftly to your aid.

Billy Graham has offered this testimony for decades, but only in recent years have we seen this testimony come full circle in his own life. He has remained faithful through the death of his beloved wife, Ruth, and has overcome many adversaries, detractors, and naysayers through the years. He is a living testimony of God's strength through a chronic disease, and he has overcome discouragement, injury, and much resistance at every turn. Dr. Graham has spoken of God's amazing grace for decades and it will ever be true. God does help us in our challenges and struggles.

Three Things to Remember

- The largest challenges we face are internal: fear, dread, weakness. When facing a large obstacle in your life or a major decision to be made, rely upon God's strength and seek God's help.

- Remember that God's answers may not come in our time or in a manner we might expect. Be open and willing to accept God's new paths or opportunities, and always pray: "Thy will be done."

- You need not face a challenge alone. There are others who care. Surround yourself with caring, considerate people who can assist you through a major struggle. And always be willing to return the favor later.

Sometimes God provides an answer. Sometimes God provides a helper. Sometimes God provides a leader. And sometimes God provides the energy and strength we need to face our own giants and overcome them. But God does provide.

Must-Know Info
Modeling Servant Leadership
By Dan Niederhofer

I t was a casual, innocent comment, but one that God would use to change the course of my life. While eating a piece of cake and mingling at a wedding reception in 1985, I found myself in a conversation with a woman who said, "Our church is looking for a youth minister to come work with our students." I heard myself respond, "I have thought about doing that. I love working with kids." Really?

I had recently graduated with a business degree and had dreams of playing football professionally, or if that didn't happen, my backup plan was to follow the path of my father and older brother into the oil industry. But the previous two summers spent as a counselor at a Christian sports camp, had planted a seed—one that I really didn't even realize was growing in me—a love of kids.

I have never had so much fun in my life than at camp! Coaching kids in football and teaching them about Jesus became a dream job for me. And so when the suggestion came, my reply came from the heart. Looking back, it is easy to see that God's ways were not my ways! And with a few twists and turns, now almost twenty-five years later, that innocent comment has led me on an adventure in ministry that has been an incredible ride.

I have experienced the huge ups and downs that come with
the territory. There have been some sleepless nights spent praying for kids or engaged with them in deep conversations about
life. There have been many changes in approaches to ministry;
new and more creative ways of reaching out to students. The days
of using an overhead projector and transparencies for songs are
long gone, but the one thing that has never changed is the rela-
tional aspect. Youth ministry isn't rocket science—in fact, as I
learned during my summer camp experience, it is really about
three things: loving students unconditionally, letting them see
Jesus living in you, and inspiring them to do the same.

Now that sounds simple, but when you try to live it out, it can
be very challenging.

Loving Students

A flood of memories and faces of specific students come to
mind—Kevin and Adam, Jerrod and Michelle, Natalie and
Ryan—so many more. God brought these students our way, and
through time, they were intertwined into the fabric of our lives.
As God continues to bring new kids our way each year at Oak
Hills Church in San Antonio, Texas, a group of volunteers have
been assembled who also possess the passion and gifts for loving
students. God has allowed our Student Ministries team to do several things really well. Because a foundation of grace has been
laid in our church, one of the best things we do is accept students
where they are with unconditional love. What does that look
like?

Each Sunday morning as kids make their way into the Student

Center, we have adult volunteers and staff who are on a mission to have conversations with them. It's an amazing sight! As hundreds enter the doors, they are greeted by caring adults, whose number one task is to help them feel like they belong. It never fails. Every week I witness adults engaged in heart-to-heart conversation, then intentionally introducing their new friends to others their age or to those who go to their school. It is truly remarkable. We know that students who do not feel this is a place for them will not come back. But acceptance is just the first step.

Modeling Jesus

There is more to loving and accepting kids than being friendly. The Boys' Club volunteer or a Little League baseball coach can do that very well. The difference is in the *life* of the volunteer. Are they living in such a way that Jesus is clearly seen? Adult leaders have tremendous influence in the life of a student. With that role, of course, comes great responsibility. It also presents an enormous opportunity. I believe the volunteer leader who is walking with Christ has both the responsibility and opportunity of ushering in the presence of Jesus to a student. Nothing excites me more than to see Christ in students' lives!

Sally has invested her life in a group of girls for almost seven years. A couple of summers ago, Katie, a student from Oak Hills, attended a summer camp near San Antonio. A week later, we received a message from the camp saying Katie had accepted Christ and wanted her youth minister to know of her decision. The card she filled out had a space at the bottom for her to write the name of her youth minister. Who did she list? Sally! What an encouragement for us. That is what we have been praying for and training our leaders to do—live out their lives in such a way that they see Jesus is living in them.

Inspiring the Mission

Loving, modeling, and inspiring: the leader who loves students and models an authentic relationship with Jesus will inspire them to do the same. At Oak Hills, we are on a mission path to move our entire church to "be Jesus to their neighbors." For students, their neighbors are their classmates. They are on the campus eight to ten hours a day, five days a week, living life with their friends. We intentionally encourage them to pass on the love of Christ they have received to their friends at school—and they are gradually getting it!

One of our high school students invited five of his buddies to our camp one summer. They were not churchgoers, but they were willing to go to Colorado to hike, raft, and hang out with other students. During the course of the week, as the Holy Spirit began to do His work, the hearts of these boys began to change. Not only did they give their lives to Christ, but their friend who invited them got a glimpse of his role in the mission of being Jesus to his friends.

Servant Leadership

So here I am, beginning my tenth year as minister to students at Oak Hills. I have been very fortunate to serve in churches that loved and supported youth ministry. I have been privileged to work with senior pastors who "got it" and encouraged the efforts of volunteer leaders, staff, and parents. But never before have I been led by a senior minister with the gifts, passion, and vision of Max Lucado. I accepted this ministry position in San Antonio because of Max's vision for Oak Hills to be a city-reaching church.

Max's early years as a missionary in Rio de Janeiro, Brazil, has been the backdrop for this vision of reaching the lost with the gospel. His missionary heart has set the tone for the entire staff and church leadership to keep the focus on Jesus, not Oak Hills. It has been an honor to minister to his three daughters as they moved through middle and high school. I have also been honored to feel the support of the Lucados as involved and supportive parents of the ministry. Max's wife, Denalyn, hosted a student Bible study in their home for six years. They have been sponsors on youth ski trips, hosted pool parties and pool baptisms, provided pizza and drinks for hundreds, all done with glad hearts. Max lives what he writes and preaches, with humility and an open hand. The past twenty years under Max's leadership have brought about amazing growth to Oak Hills Church: new satellite campuses and literally thousands of changed lives for Christ. But there are a few things that haven't changed. In fact, I believe they are the foundation and reason for any "success" of Oak Hills Church.

The things that haven't changed were recently "rediscovered" in a meeting with a consulting firm that was hired to help us hone Oak Hills' city-reaching vision. The question was asked, "What have been the major turning points over the last twenty years at Oak Hills?" The staff and key ministry leaders in that meeting began to share. After an hour or so, there were three very clear findings that rose to the top. Each one related back to Max's leadership as senior minister:

- Twenty years of a humble spirit preaching the cross of Christ has laid a foundation of *grace*.
- Twenty years of patience with prayer has produced a culture ready to accept change.
- Twenty years of servant leadership has placed us in a position for a mission move outward like never before.

These qualities have made their way into every part of our church, including student ministries. Reflecting on the past makes it easy for me to see why our youth ministry has the qualities it does. For us, there is nothing more important than loving kids with the love of Christ, living in such a way that they can see Jesus, and inspiring them to pass on this love to their friends. This is our prayer and passion.

Must-Know Info
Growing a Family Ministry
By Kathryn Lay

For the past twenty-five years my husband and I have ministered to refugees and immigrants in our community. We have helped them with their English, been International Friends to college students from around the world, helped develop a refugee church, shared the gospel, and made friends with those who were hungry for an American friend in a strange land.

But even more exciting to us was how our thirteen-year-old daughter became a part of our ministry. Ministering as a family has given us opportunities to work together to share God's love, help others, learn more about one another's gifts and talents, and be a team.

Every Monday evening nearly 100 people from over a dozen countries come to the free English school that Richard and I co-direct at our church. Of the more than twenty volunteers who teach, drive buses, pray, coordinate, babysit, and make friends with our students and their families, our daughter, Michelle, is the youngest. She is part of the morning preparations as we arrive early to set up classrooms, make copies of lessons and roll sheets, and set up registration tables. She looks forward each week to her time as helper in the childcare room, where children from infants through early elementary age are cared for while their parents learn and improve their English.

Some of the children have little-to-no English language skills, but Michelle's love and gentleness draws small and sometimes very frightened children to her as she cares for them, makes them laugh, and helps to ease their fears while they are away from their parents.

On these school nights, our family time together is often hectic and separate, but we value one another in the roles that God has placed us in. Michelle has learned to care for all people, regardless of skin color, language, or customs. Even at the age of ten she was a valuable part of our ministry team and had a place in sharing God's love to others. Years later, her experience, skills, loving heart, and open personality have made her a true minister in her own right.

Others have found that ministering as a family grows long-lasting and endless opportunities to draw closer to one another as they serve God together.

Every summer Dean and Pam Rowell, along with their two children, chaperone youth groups that travel with Volunteer Christian Builders. They also participate in service trips with their church's youth to minister in Arkansas, Tennessee, Missouri, Alaska, Louisiana, Texas, Colorado, Mexico, and Wyoming. Their children have been a part of these mission trips since they were babies, even celebrating birthdays while on their family ministry vacations. They have gone on building trips and helped to construct buildings for churches in pioneer areas, as well as on trips to teach Bible schools, witness at fairs, lead worship services, paint churches, do park ministries, and more. Their children, ages fourteen and eight, love these family trips.

Pam feels that one of the benefits to a family ministering together is setting an example for their children to follow. "It shows that a family can serve together. To see one of your children stretched to meet a need is such an affirmation of the way they are being taught."

Ministering as a family can be weekly, as our ministry is, long distance as with the Rowells, or local without a lengthy time commitment as with James and Selena.

James, Selena, and their sons Brandon, fourteen, and Austin, twelve, share food and friendship with lonely, discouraged, and needy people at their local shelter. One Sunday night a month for the last six years, they have taken food, prepared it, and served it to the homeless. They help where needed, whether it is setting up for the evening meal, greeting and watching the people as they come through the metal detector, praying with the women's Bible study group, or cleaning up afterwards.

"The kids didn't really know about homeless people and that there were people who did not have food," Selena says. "It shows them that there are less fortunate people in our city and that Jesus wants us to help others."

Like the rest of the families who serve together, Selena feels this helps her children see there are ways to help others less fortunate, even in seemingly simple ways.

You don't have to be a full-time minister, seminary student, or spiritual giant to serve others in Christ's name.

Some families have made it a tradition to minister at local

shelters or ministries for the poor during the holiday time; helping to serve meals, sort donated gifts and clothing, wrap gifts to send overseas or to local orphanages, and more.

There are times when we are tired, and the thought of a long Monday evening seems unbearable after a busy weekend and Monday at school and work. Yet we find ourselves rejuvenated when our students come to class, sharing their fears and joys, thanking us for how we've helped them. And every week Michelle is seeing God work in big and small ways.

My prayer is that someday, the seeds we plant will become a huge field of blessings to those we minister to and in our memories. And, that someday as well, Michelle will grow her own family ministry.

Tips for Growing Your Own Family Ministry

- **Tilling the soil.** Pray as a family about your future ministry, about how you can develop or become involved in a ministry as a family. Make a list of ministry possibilities that you feel drawn toward. Pray for God's leading to a ministry that appeals to you as a family, one you feel God is calling you to do, or that matches your talents and gifts. Think about your time commitment. If you are already overly busy, you may decide it's time to cut other activities for this very worthwhile one.

- **Planting.** Involve the whole family. If anyone has concerns, address them. Talk with other families doing the same thing. Make a commitment to God as a family and begin praying for the ones you will be ministering to and with.

- **Watering.** Become involved with your new ministry. Find ways to learn and to bless others. Find ways to include your own spiritual gifts and talents.
- **Weeding.** Expect conflict and opposition from spiritual forces, family, or friends who don't understand your calling, including your children. Share frustrations with one another and with your ministry team. Don't let frustrations fester into discouragement. Pray for wisdom to overcome problems.
- **Harvesting.** Get to know the people you are ministering to and pray for them as a family. Show God's love as you serve. As a family, share the exciting things that are happening in the ministry.

Just as God helps each of us to grow stronger spiritually, together families can grow stronger as we care about others around us.

Must-Know Info
Fat and Sassy, Spiritually Speaking
By Elaine L. Bridge

My husband needed to gain weight after losing almost thirty-five pounds as a result of radiation treatments directed at his throat. Those of us who struggle on a daily basis to keep from packing on extra pounds have trouble relating to the struggle he's gone through to put lost weight back on. I admit to expressing exasperation myself when one day he asked me in desperation what I thought he could do to reverse the losing trend he was experiencing. I looked at him and said (probably in a louder voice and with more force than was necessary) three simple words in response: "Stuff your face!"

It seemed so easy to me: simply eat at any and every opportunity. But such advice was not as easily put into practice. There were other factors to consider. He experienced very real pain when swallowing; not just in his throat but in his ears. He had a dry mouth brought on by the damage to his salivary glands. Dining became a much longer and more difficult process than it used to be. But lack of appetite seemed to be the biggest enemy to his weight gain. He had simply lost his interest in food and had to force himself to eat. His stomach had shrunk to the point that just a small amount of food would fill him up completely.

Many of us experience similar problems on a spiritual level as we try to grow in the Lord. Spiritual weight gain is our goal, whether it's to gain back ground we lost in some battle we faced, or simply that we wish to increase our muscle mass to prepare ourselves for upcoming skirmishes with the enemy. We know what we want to gain; it's the process of achieving the goal that's the challenge. We may have tried several approaches in the past, none of which achieved the desired results. In desperation we may finally come to the Lord and ask for His help. His answer to us might be as simple as my response to my husband: Stuff your face (spiritually speaking).

Easier said than done. But perhaps there are some spiritual principles we can learn to help us in this endeavor by looking at some parallels in the physical realm. Gaining weight in the physical world is accomplished when we take in more calories than we expend during the day. Active people burn more calories than those whose lifestyles are more sedentary. In the same way, those who are regularly engaging the enemy in battle will need to spend more time in worship, in prayer, and in the Word to stay ahead of the fight. Those who neglect to do so are eventually worn down by the continual onslaught of the enemy until they no longer have the strength to fight.

"No pain, no gain" is a commonly heard phrase that indicates that physical goals are achieved through the passage of painful progress. Spiritual goals are often achieved the same way. Spending more time in the presence of the Lord may cost us something. The first thing that might have to go is pride. We simply have to admit that we can't accomplish this on our own and humble ourselves enough to ask God for help. The answers He gives us may be hard to swallow at first, causing real pain as they tramp across sore spots in our relationship with Him. Yet these areas have to be dealt with and the pain endured if we're ever to experience real growth.

Some of us have been spiritually dry for a long time. Just as a plant suffering from drought needs a lot of water poured on it a little at a time, so we need to soak ourselves slowly in the Living Water we're offered. Too much at once causes wasteful runoff. We have to absorb truth a little at a time to see the growth we desire. Drinking in the presence of God may therefore require more time than we've been prone to devote to it in the past. We may have to let go of other pursuits to make time in our lives for what's really important.

Perhaps the greatest problem we deal with in growing spiritually is simply a lack of interest in the food that's set before us. We seem to have lost our taste for that which we know we need to consume in order to grow. Our Bible study times may be boring instead of full of the mind-blowing revelations other people seem to experience. It's important to note that these other people probably didn't start out on fire right from the start, either. But they developed a taste for spiritual things by starting small and gradually increasing their consumption as they increased their appetite. Soon they found that they were *hungry* for the food God set before them each day, and they began to approach their spiritual mealtimes with eager anticipation, anxious to see what God had on the menu for them each time they came to the table.

Sometimes monitoring your progress can help. My husband

posted a piece of paper on the wall above our bathroom scale on which he recorded his weight after stepping on the scale each morning. Some days he found he'd gained weight from the day before, other days he'd lost a pound or two. Looking at the day-to-day progress, he sometimes became discouraged because he saw so little change. But viewed from beginning to end, he could see a steady weight gain overall.

I started using a prayer journal to monitor my spiritual progress when I first got serious in my pursuit of a greater spiritual life. Every day I'd record what I learned in my devotional times. The occasional blank pages could be distressing, but when I looked back through the book after a period of some weeks or months, I was amazed at the quantity of spiritual ground I'd covered. I found the record to be a real encouragement to me as I continued to make progress.

At one point my husband began to realize that a little exercise might help the process along. Months of relative inactivity as he dealt with the side effects of his treatments had caused loss of muscle tone. We, too, need to exercise our faith as it grows within our spirits, mindful to develop muscle and not just spiritual fat cells from too much inactivity in the spiritual realm. The Bible admonishes us to be *doers* of the Word, and not hearers only (James 1:22).

The most important thing is to not give up. I was saddened one morning to see the sheet of paper on which my husband had been recording his weight gain thrown in the trash. On the same day, he asked me to look into returning the unused cans of nutritional supplement that he had remaining. It seemed to me that because his progress hadn't been happening fast enough to please him he was simply giving up on the process. He'd just stay the weight he was and not worry about it any longer. Yet I couldn't help but notice that his clothes still hung on him and his arms and legs were still painfully thin.

Don't be satisfied with the present circumstances in your spiritual life. Whether you're just starting out or have been actively pursuing God for some time, there will always be more mountains to climb, more ground to gain, more spiritual strength to be developed so that more battles can be won. God sees us as He knows we can be, and it must disturb Him greatly to see us content to stay in our present state when He knows what we can become spiritually if we'll just keep our noses to the grindstone and stay hungry for more of Him.

The Writers

Linda E. Allen travels to Bolivia annually with the VIM team from her church. She enjoys sharing her Bolivian experiences and blessings in her writing. Linda can be contacted at lindaeallen@sbcglobal.net.

Rachel Allord is a freelance writer, pastor's wife, and mother living in central Wisconsin. Her stories have appeared in Chicken Soup for the Soul books and her devotionals have appeared in various publications.

Diana M. Amadeo is an award-winning author who has in excess of 450 publications. Her works have appeared in six Chicken Soup for the Soul anthologies, four children's books, and a diverse collection of magazines, newspapers, and anthologies.

Sara Joy Baker is a retired special-education teacher and a pastor's wife. They have three grown children, four grandchildren, and five great grandchildren. Sara loves to sing and is involved with community theater and the local senior center.

Edna Bell-Pearson is the author of *Fragile Hopes, Transient Dreams and other Stories*. Bell-Pearson's short stories, articles, essays, and poems have appeared in over a hundred magazines and newspapers nationwide. She is a member of Kansas Center for the Book, Kansas Author's Club, and Author's Den.

Carol M. Benthal-Bingley lives in Rockford, Illinois with her husband and three daughters. She is an artist, mother, runner, and founder of Annie's Locker (http://www.annieslocker.org), a non-profit that collects and distributes new and used fitness gear to people in need. She is proud that "Running for Two" has blossomed into a ministry that serves others. Several years ago, God gave her these words: *Create. Inspire.* That's what she strives to do. Write to her at carol@b2design.com

Pam Bostwick has many articles appearing in Christian magazines, newspapers, and anthologies, including *The Ultimate Teacher*. She enjoys her country home, loves the beach, plays guitar, and is a volunteer counselor. Legally blind and hearing-impaired, Pam has seven children and ten grandchildren, and happily remarried 7/7/07.

Elaine L. Bridge worked in the woods on the west coast as a forester before becoming a stay-at-home mom to her three boys. Now living in Ohio, she works part-time in a grocery store and is devoted to developing her relationship with God, caring for her family, and writing inspirational material.

Nicole Bromley is a professional speaker and the author of *Hush: Moving from Silence to Healing After Childhood Sexual Abuse* and *Breathe: Finding Freedom to Thrive in Relationships After Childhood Sexual Abuse*. Nicole is the founder and director of OneVOICE enterprises (www.onevoiceenterprises.com).

Susan Dollyhigh is a freelance writer and columnist, and a contributing author in *Spirit and Heart: A Devotional Journey* and *Faith and Finances: In God We Trust*. Her articles and devotionals have appeared in *Connection Magazine*, *The Upper Room* and *The Secret*

Place. She is also a contributing online writer for ChristianDevotions.us, Internet-Cafedevotions and TheChristianPulse.

Terri Elders, LCSW, is recently widowed and feels blessed to be comforted by two dogs and three cats at her country home near Colville, Washington. She has been published in multiple anthologies, including Chicken Soup for the Soul, Cup of Comfort, Ultimate, and others. Write her: telders@hotmail.com.

Alyssa Fanara is a freshman in high school who plays piano and guitar. She has always loved writing, music, and art, and her current writing project is about 400 pages long and counting.

Kristen Feola is a freelance writer in Springfield, Missouri. She and her husband would like to take more trips to Yosemite together, but are busy raising their daughters and teaching them "the ropes." In her spare time, Kristen is working on a book about the Daniel Fast and posting recipes on her blog www.thosewhohunger.blogspot.com.

Barbara J. Fisher is the author of *Stolen Moments* and a contributor to nine Chicken Soup books. In 2007 she was the editor of two anthologies, *Voices of Alcohol* and *Voices of Lung Cancer*. She has published two children books, *How Much Can Teddy Bear?* and *Nobody's Lion*. She has been published internationally in magazines such as *Woman's World*, *Guideposts*, and *Messenger of the Sacred Heart*. She and her husband Joe live in Fremont, Ohio, where she owns her own bookstore.

Lisa Finch lives in Forest, Ontario with her wonderful husband, Chris, and their three beautiful children, Hailey, Matthew, and Ben. Her work has been published in three anthologies: *Living the Serenity Prayer*, *The Ultimate Cat Lover*, and *Christmas Traditions*. Visit her at http://www.finchtales.webs.com.

Kathy Fitzgerald is a writer and mom who tries to introduce a little religion into her life each day. She lives with her husband and daughter in Edmonton, Alberta, Canada.

Valerie J. Frost serves at Horizon Christian Fellowship in San Diego, California. She and her husband, Terry, are the parents of three grown children. They have nine energetic grandchildren and two turbo-charged Jack Russell terriers, Daphne and Rocket. Publishing credits include Legacy Publishing, Cook Communications, *Decision Magazine*, and Chicken Soup for the Soul anthologies.

Lynne Gentry has been married to a pastor for twenty-nine years. She serves her church as the Director of Creative Arts. An inspirational speaker, she performs monologues from her original work, Save Momma. She has published several articles in *Christian Woman* magazine and a short story in *God Sightings*.

Judy Lee Green is an award-winning writer and speaker whose spirit and roots reach deep into the Appalachian Mountains. Tennessee-bred and cornbread-fed, she has been published hundreds of times and received dozens of awards for her work. Her colorful Southern family is the source for much of her poetry and prose. She lives in the rolling hills of Middle Tennessee.

Kathryn Heckenbach is a freelance writer and aspiring novelist, with personal essays appearing in Sunday school periodicals and short fiction published in several online magazines. A graduate of the University of Tampa, she is also an artist and home school mom.

Jerry Hendrick works for the State of Michigan as an adult foster care licensing consultant. He also teaches social work courses at Grand Valley State University and is the men's tennis coach at Aquinas College. Jerry has been married to his wife, Beth, for twenty-two years, and together they have three children; Ashley, Aaron, and Austin. The Hendricks reside in Grand Rapids, Michigan, and continue to post updates on Ashley's hospital-sponsored CarePage website. These writings can be found at www.carepages.com, patient name, AshleyHendrick.

Jeanne R. Hill is an author, an inspirational speaker, and a contributing editor to *Guideposts* magazine. Her award-winning short stories and articles are often chosen for anthologies. She has authored monthly columns in magazines and published two inspirational books: *Daily Breath* and *Secrets of Prayer Joy.*

Teresa Hoy lives and writes in the country with her husband and large fur family of cats and dogs. Read more of her work in *The Ultimate Cat Lover* and *Chicken Soup for the Soul: What I Learned from the Cat.* Visit her at http://www.teresahoy.com.

Jewell Johnson lives in Arizona with her husband, LeRoy. They are parents to six children and grandparents to nine. Besides writing, Jewel enjoys walking, reading. and quilting.

Nan Trammell Jones is thankful for the opportunity God has provided her to develop a long-awaited speaking and writing ministry called Jubilant Light Ministries. She has a burden for women who are struggling with their faith and need to be reminded of God's unconditional love. Visit her at www.jubilantlight.com.

Mimi Greenwood Knight is a freelance writer living in South Louisiana with her husband, David, and their three children. Mimi has more than 300 articles in print and tales in a couple dozen anthologies including fifteen Chicken Soup for the Soul anthologies, *The Ultimate Mom, The Ultimate Dog Lover,* and *The Ultimate Teacher.*

Nikki Loftin is an award-winning freelance writer, former teacher, and family ministry director. She lives and writes near Austin, Texas, with her Scottish husband, two rowdy sons, two dogs, and five chickens. Comments are welcome on her website: www.nikkiloftin.com.

Linda Mehus-Barber lives with her husband, two dogs, and a cat in the seaside community of Crescent Beach in Surrey, British Columbia. She teaches English and ancient history at Regent Christian Academy where she can freely share her faith with her seventh-grade students.

Pierre O'Rourke worked as an artist, firefighter, celebrity interviewer, maitre d', columnist, publicist, and authored a media guide to best-selling authors and celebrities while he tried to figure what he wanted to be when he grew up. They urged him to write books. It only took a dozen years for him to listen and take action. He writes in Scottsdale, Arizona, with his furry pal Nubble. Neither have plans to grow up anytime soon. Visit Pierre at www.pierre-orourke.com.

Ava Pennington is a writer, speaker, and Bible teacher. She has published magazine articles and contributed to seventeen anthologies. She is also author of *One Year Alone with God: 366 Devotions on the Names of God.* Learn more at http://www.AvaWrites.com.

Kay Presto is a motorsports journalist and photographer who has covered all types of racing. She has also covered racing for ESPN *Speedweek* and CNN, has done public relations for race teams, and has an international website: www.carsandcompetition.com. She has received sixty-nine national and state awards for her work and is a professional speaker. She can be reached at prestoprod6@yahoo.com

Kelli Regan is thankful for the freedom Jesus offers and passionately shares that message through writing, Bible study, and prison ministry. She's authored numerous articles and lives in Bucks County, Pennsylvania, with her husband and two children. She shares her insights and adventures on her blog, Awesome God, Ordinary Girl at www.awesomegodordinarygirl.blogspot.com.

Carol McAdoo Rehme's life has been blessed by teachers and preachers, chaplains and pastors, bishops and lay ministers. She shares her experiences through writing and speaking. A freelance editor/author, Carol has coauthored five gift books and compiled several anthologies. Learn more at www.rehme.com.

Mark Sanders, LCSW, CADC, is a member of the faculty of Governors State University in Illinois. He has done presentations throughout the U.S., Europe, Canada, and the Caribbean islands, and is the author of four books and numerous workbooks.

Michael Jordan Segal, MSW was shot in the head as an innocent bystander to a robbery and then defied all odds by first surviving, and then returning to college, earning two degrees with honors, and marrying his high-school sweetheart, Sharon. They have a daughter, Shawn. Mike is a social worker at Memorial Hermann Hospital, and an author and a motivational speaker. A CD of his twelve inspirational stories is available at his website: www.InspirationByMike.com.

Benjamin Snow is the pseudonym for a South Florida writer who enjoys sharing the stories of his childhood. Having honed his storytelling skills over his years of service in the military, Ben now prefers to put them on paper to be shared someday with his grandchildren.

Cynthia Stiverson's call to ministry has opened doors to speak at conferences, retreats, and in churches throughout the U.S. and in South Africa. She is a contributing writer to *Breathe* and *Pearl Girls*. As founder of WOVEN, she authored two workbooks. She resides in Howard, Ohio, with her husband, Mark. Visit her at http://www.CynthiaStiverson.com.

Annmarie B. Tait resides in Conshohocken, Pennsylvania, with her husband, Joe, and "Sammy the Wonder Yorkie." In addition to writing stories about her large Irish-Catholic family and the memories they made, Annmarie enjoys singing and recording Irish and American folk songs. Contact Annmarie at irishbloom@aol.com.

Patricia Taylor and her husband James are authors of *On the Wings of the Wind*, and live in San Antonio, Texas. Since retiring from the U.S. Army Chaplain Corps, James has served as a Lutheran interim pastor in several congregations. Pat shares his ministry through her gifts of compassion, visitation, and speaking.

Shaundra Taylor is a mountain mama, spiritual renegade, spin addict, and burgeoning freelancer who endeavors to share her wonder at the elements of truth and grace in the everyday world around her. Her blog is Musin' Mama: Life at the Speed of Wonder at musinmama.blogspot.com.

Cristy Trandahl works as a freelance writer while raising her six children. Cristy's stories are published in dozens of nationally distributed magazine and anthologies. See www.cristytrandahl.com.

Cheryl Elaine Williams is a postal retiree living in Pittsburgh, Pennsylvania. She recently underwent successful surgery for a complete thyroidectomy due to a diagnosis of a malignant nodule on the thyroid. She credits prayer and the support of her family, friends, and faith community in helping her to face this challenge in a positive and life-affirming manner.

The Photographers

Lorrie Keip Cositore is the director of continuing education for U.S. Journal Training, which specializes in providing educational opportunities for mental health professionals through conferences and online home study. Lorrie's faith has always sustained her when faced with life's challenges, and the photo she submitted serves as a reminder that her faith need not be great or deep for God's love to support her; it need only be the size of a mustard seed.

Jennifer Crites is a Honolulu-based photographer and writer whose words and images exploring travel, contemporary lifestyles, food, education, and science have been published in magazines and books worldwide, including *The Ultimate Gardener* and *The Ultimate Bird Lover*. Enjoy more of Jennifer's work at http://www.jennifer critesphotography.com.

Sandy Dolan, a third generation Floridian, is dedicated to preserving the State's architectural and natural heritage through her fine art photography. From the seashore and coastal islands to the inland Everglades, Sandy captures the unique beauty of Florida. Her photographs of historical landmarks, scenic landscapes, lush foliage, and tropical birds are intended to inspire an appreciation for preservation and encourage protection for our natural environment.

Marie Franqui is a poet, scholar, and multimedia artist. Marie lives in Wilmington, North Carolina with her two great loves: Alexander and Kong. When not photographing the splendor of her world, Marie occupies herself by writing, traveling, and playing her favorite game: *Where in the World is Marlee Binks?*

Paula Jansen's goal as a commercial photographer is to illustrate her client's vision in the most artistic and creative way possible. Paula uses a mixture of natural and strobe light to render objects in a life-like manner. She began her career working on children's books and enjoys collaborating on projects with art directors and editors. Her photography is featured in *Sharing the Table at Garland's Lodge*, which was a 2006 Finalist for the IACP Cookbook Award. Please visit Paula's website, http://www. paulajansen.com, to enjoy more of her photography and her visual blog.

The Must-Know Experts

J. Brent Bill is a writer, photographer, retreat leader, and Quaker minister. Brent is recognized as one of the most important communicators of the spirituality of the Quaker tradition today. He's been called "a substantial spiritual guide, but never in a flashy way . . . perhaps something like Mister Rogers Meets the Dalai Lama." He is the author and co-author of many books, including *Sacred Compass: The Way of Spiritual Discernment* and *Holy Silence: The Gift of Quaker Spirituality*, in addition to more than 100 short stories and non-fiction articles. He also is the author of the popular blog HolyOrdinary (holyordinary.blogspot.com). He can be reached at http://www.brentbill.com

Elaine L. Bridge worked in the woods on the west coast as a forester before becoming a stay-at-home mom to her three boys. Now living in Ohio, she works part-time in a grocery store and is devoted to developing her relationship with God, caring for her family, and writing inspirational material.

Gaye Clark is a full-time wife, mother of two teens, a part-time nurse, and a freelance writer. She currently leads a ministry of racial reconciliation called Women United in Christ in the inner city of Augusta, Georgia.

Kurt Johnston has been in youth ministry for more than twenty years and is still smiling! Since 1997, Kurt has served as the Junior High Pastor at Saddleback Church in Lake Forest, California. Kurt is also an author, speaker, and founder of simplyjuniorhigh.com, a company dedicated to creating quality resources for others who work with young teens. Kurt has been married to his wife, Rachel, for eighteen years and together they have two children, Kayla and Cole. In their free time the Johnstons enjoy heading to the desert to ride dirt bikes.

Kathryn Lay is a full-time author and writer living in Texas with her husband of thirty years, her daughter, and her dogs. For many years she and her family ministered together and now, her daughter is old enough to minister on her own with her friends. It is exciting to see that she continues to care for others as she gets older. Kathryn spends her time writing children's books, magazine pieces, and essays as well as speaking to school kids and participating in various ministries at her church. She has written a book for writers as well, *The Organized Writer is a Selling Writer* and teaches online writing classes. Visit her website at http://www.kathrynlay.com to learn more about her writing and speaking, or contact her at rlay15@aol.com.

Dr. Linda McCoy began her professional career as a secondary school French teacher and entered ministry as a second career. Linda holds a bachelor and master's degrees from Indiana University, a master of divinity (magna cum laude) from Christian Theological Seminary, and a doctor of ministry from United Theological Seminary in Dayton, Ohio. Linda was named one of the "Most Influential Women" in Indianapolis in 2008. In 1995 she founded The Garden—a pioneer ministry in a multi-site approach that has proven meaningful to the more than 1,200 people who call it their spiritual home. This unique ministry can be found at http://thegardenonline.org. Linda has authored three books: *It's News to Me: Messages of Hope for Those Who Have Not Heard, Planting a Garden,* and *Igniting Worship.*

Dan Niederhofer serves Oak Hills Church as Minister to Students. With almost twenty-five years of ministry experience and a God-given passion for students, he leads a team of staff and volunteers in reaching out to students and their friends by developing friendships in an atmosphere of unconditional acceptance, love, and grace. Married for twenty-five years to Janet, who teaches first grade, Dan has four sons, ages 21, 19, 16, and 10. He is also a volunteer for Young Life and currently leads the Churchill High School Club.

William H. Willimon has been a Bishop of The United Methodist Church since 2004. He leads the 157,000 Methodists and 792 pastors in North Alabama. For twenty years he was Dean of the Chapel and Professor of Christian Ministry at Duke University, Durham, North Carolina. He is the author of sixty books which have sold a combined total of more than one million copies. His articles have appeared in many publications, including *The Christian Ministry, Quarterly Review, Liturgy, Worship,* and *Christianity Today.* He has written curriculum materials and video for youth, young adults, and adults, and is editor-at-large for *The Christian Century.* His *Pulpit Resource* is used each week by over 8,000 pastors in the U.S., Canada, and Australia.

The Author

Todd Outcalt is a pastor, speaker, and writer. He is the author of twenty books, including *The Best Things In Life Are Free* and *The Healing Touch*. Other titles include *Before You Say "I Do," Your Beautiful Wedding on Any Budget*, and *$5 Youth Ministry*. Todd has also written for many magazines, including *Leadership, Rev!*, and *The Christian Century*.

Since 2004, Todd has pastored Calvary United Methodist Church in Brownsburg, Indiana—a large, growing congregation near Indianapolis. In 2005, he preached for twelve hours—the longest sermon in Indiana history—and for the past three years he has blogged daily on humorous subjects related to reading and writing.

Todd enjoys hiking, kayaking, and reading great novels. He lives in Brownsburg with his wife of twenty-five years and his two children. Read more in his blog at http://www.toddoutcalt.blogspot.com.

Copyright Credits

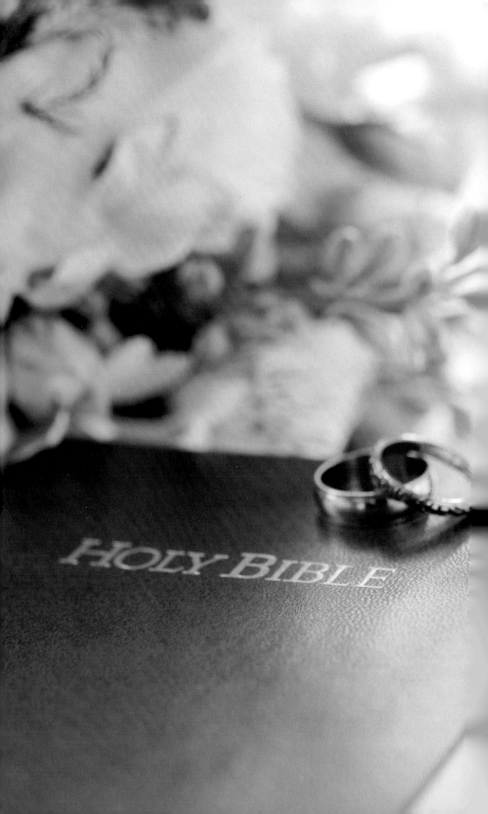